ADAPTATION STRATEGIES FOR INTERIOR ARCHITECTURE AND DESIGN

Bloomsbury Visual Arts
An imprint of Bloomsbury Publishing Plc

Imprint previously known as AVA Publishing

50 Bedford Square   1385 Broadway
London   New York
WC1B 3DP   NY 10018
UK   USA

www.bloomsbury.com

BLOOMSBURY VISUAL ARTS, BLOOMSBURY and the Diana logo are trademarks of Bloomsbury Publishing Plc

British Library Cataloguing-in-Publication Data
A catalogue record for this book is available from the British Library.

ISBN:
PB: 978-1-4725-6713-0
ePDF: 978-1-4725-6958-5

Library of Congress Cataloging-in-Publication Data
Names: Brooker, Graeme, author.
Title: Adaptation strategies for interior architecture and design / Graeme
  Brooker.
Description: New York : Bloomsbury Visual Arts, 2016. | Series: Required reading
  range | Includes bibliographical references and index.
Identifiers: LCCN 2015044115| ISBN 9781472567130 (paperback) | ISBN
  9781472569585 (epdf)
Subjects: LCSH: Interior architecture. | Interior decoration. |
  Buildings--Remodeling for other use. | BISAC: ARCHITECTURE / Adaptive
  Reuse & Renovation. | ARCHITECTURE / General. | ARCHITECTURE / Interior
  Design / General.
Classification: LCC NA2850 .B745 2016 | DDC 729--dc23 LC record available at http://lccn.loc.gov/2015044115

Series: Required Reading Range

Cover design: Louise Dugdale
Cover image: David Kohn Architects / José Hevia Blach

Typeset by Hoop Design
Printed and bound in China

ADAPTATION STRATEGIES FOR INTERIOR ARCHITECTURE AND DESIGN

GRAEME BROOKER

BLOOMSBURY VISUAL ARTS
AN IMPRINT OF BLOOMSBURY PUBLISHING PLC

BLOOMSBURY
LONDON · OXFORD · NEW YORK · NEW DELHI · SYDNEY

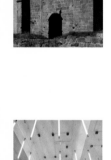

As those who study and practice well know, design is a complex process. In the past three decades, reworking the existing built environment has emerged as a central challenge. Designers are increasingly called upon to facilitate equitable adaptation. Mr. Brooker is a pragmatist, and in many ways, the timing of his book is impeccable. It is a privilege to introduce Adaption Strategies for Interior Architecture and Design—an introduction to process-oriented design strategies for practical and humanistic functions. The author concisely designates eight design strategies, with special emphasis on interiority, and each is presented in a manner to assist the designer to make important decisions about the form and organization of building sites, structures, and elements; reaching far beyond the simple acts of refurbishment or expansion. Each section begins with a clear definition and explanation of the strategy, and its relevance to design. Full-scale built examples play a special role in illustrating how a selection of stylish and engaging projects actually came into being.

In a book such as this, brevity is indispensable to its readership. Vast concepts are distilled into a comprehensive summation to inscribe new design into existing conditions. Effectively, the author points out that resourcefulness is more significant to the quality of design than any particular resource, and although he does not, by any means, suggest the subordination of modern design to remnants of the past, a convincing argument is made that modernism achieves some of its best results in the minority position. In recognition of the designer's inclination toward idiosyncratic inventions, the book presents and illustrates the use of strategies, such as "Intervention," "Insertion," and "On/Off Site," and others deployed elsewhere, including "Installation," "Artifice,"

and "Narrative." The latter set comprises a relatively continuous and fleeting set of strategies, perhaps more easily overlooked. "Reprogramming" is defined as a strategy to achieve continued use, by reinvigorating abandoned or otherwise inaccessible environs; in essence, this approach to design is working "within," rather than "on," a project. "Superuse" defines maximum use of surplus materials, to capture "resonant meanings," an elusive concept clever exemplifies in a project using second-hand clothing to fabricate new, freestanding auditorium partitions. Divested of its original structure and function, the leftover fabric calls into question the meaning of a wall. Still other functions are questioned in the redesign of an abandoned complex of old stone buildings and a relic of bygone urban infrastructure.

Adaption Strategies for Interior Architecture and Design is a sound resource for design students, practicing professionals, educators and researchers. Novice designers may find it useful to revisit various sections, over time, to consolidate a thorough understanding of these basic complex processes; reflect upon progress, and identify challenges on the horizon. Within the text, the author includes additional sources to consider. Practicing designers and educators are likely to discover the value in this framework to capture implicit knowledge in planning and design, to protect and preserve our environments, as a means to achieve sustainability: wellbeing and quality of life for ourselves and future generations.

George Ranalli, FAIA is an American architect based in New York, and Dean of CUNY.

Anne Valentino, PhD, is a clinical psychologist based in New York.

"Anything and everything is available for conversion—there is no building that is *a priori* unfit for conversion. The future in planning and design lies above all in the area of the existing mass product."[1]

Adaptation Strategies for Interior Architecture and Design outlines a number of different approaches utilized when redesigning interior space when reusing existing buildings. This book proposes that there are a series of very particular processes that are based upon the responses to a space that is or has been outlined for new occupation. These processes are exemplified by a series of strategies, employed by the designer, in an attempt to filter and synthesize a mixture of information, ideas, and resources in order to form a new, clear, and meaningful spatial design. This book demonstrates how design strategies are used to enable and articulate design ideas. These types of procedures require a very particular and specific sensibility; one that promotes an awareness and responsiveness to existing contexts, and one that advocates a willingness to accept, edit and reform existing or about to exist space. In this book, I propose the idea that the design of the interior is often reliant upon the understanding of what is already present. Whether a drawing on a page or on a computer screen, or whether the envelope of an existing building, interior architecture, design, and decoration are the disciplines that are based upon the understanding of what already exists in order to then formulate and craft something new. This book summarizes and, using a series of exemplary contemporary case studies, presents a series of unique and innovative strategies that respond to what is already present, in order to make something new.

Adaptation Strategies for Interior Architecture and Design outlines a number of primary reuse strategies in order to act as a primer for the subject. It will also introduce readers to recombinant cultures, methods, and processes that will explore the importance of context in both its site-specific and cultural meaning. It will examine a number of approaches that show how the adaptation of the existing and, in particular, old buildings, as opposed to new builds, can provide unique and unusual transformative solutions for the historic and the contemporary built environment. It uses the images and drawings of a series of case studies of recent projects in order to demonstrate each strategy. Each strategy is contextualized with an introduction that explains what it means, sometimes using other creative and spatially related fields such as installation art, painting, sculpture, and furniture design, in order to demonstrate how reuse is prevalent in all other creative disciplines.

Each strategy has five exemplary and current case studies drawn from around the world. This broad, international representation reflects the global emergence of building reuse as a sustainable and effective built environment strategy and shows how this type of work has become one of the most valuable and contemporary forms of making the built environment. As Liz Diller states: "This notion of reinventing infrastructure, rethinking what we already have, has caught the public imagination."[2]

Strategy

"What makes it so difficult to describe building conversion is that it is not enough simply to present the final result. A building conversion involves a complex interaction between old and new, before and after, and all points in-between, including a strategy, until it eventually reaches the end stage."[3]

Derived from military planning, *strategy* denotes a plan to achieve a goal, often under conditions of uncertainty. Working with the existing will always require a plan, often one that incorporates uncertainties, and contingencies, particularly in relation to what a designer might find on-site when work commences. The strategies described in this book reflect this and incorporate the ambiguity of these types of approaches to building reuse by utilizing terms that are fluid yet which relate to particular actions undertaken when transforming the built environment. The strategies are not singular and will sometimes, to a more or lesser extent, be used in conjunction with each other, emphasizing their fluid nature. But each strategy demonstrates a unique approach to building reuse, when not "starting from scratch."

Strategies are usually realized through the deployment of tactics or *devices*. The devices or instruments of interiors are elements such as walls, floors, ceilings, and soffits (both found and imposed surfaces); objects such as furniture or larger items such as pavilions; forms of movement such as stairs, lifts, walkways, bridges, corridors; and openings such as doors and windows (both made and existing and both natural and artificial light). These devices are not the focus of this book but they will be used to explain and detail the chosen manifestations of strategy in each of the case studies.

A single chapter represents each of the eight strategies that are outlined in this book. Eight strategies are chosen in order to exemplify the primary ideas involved in reworking the existing. They are not exhaustive, but it is the author's view that the eight describe and formulate a substantial range of strategical responses to the reuse of existing buildings. They summarize and draw together key themes and ideas, such as recycling, sustainability, temporality, continuity, layering, and so on, embodying a language that is prevalent in the interior discipline. Because the design of the interior often deals with the "extant," whether built or yet to be built, many of the approaches toward its processes are embedded in ideas about understanding the existing, such as alteration, reworking, and transformation. In essence, working with the existing is quite a different approach to starting with a clean slate, an approach that advocates a tabula rasa methodology or starting from scratch. Therefore, each of the eight strategies demonstrates an approach to creating interior space that is not defined by function but instead is based on the response to the existing building. This is an important and unique distinction for the book. When reusing existing buildings, a functionalist ideology is rendered ambiguous when a designated building is repurposed for a different use, one that it was never intended for. Therefore it is often counterproductive to categorize interior projects by function, when, in reality, it is really the "possession" and "occupation" of space through reprogramming that is the most useful distinction.

Each of the eight chapters in the book is titled with one of the primary strategies. They are:

1   Reprogramming
2   Intervention
3   Superuse
4   Artifice
5   Installation
6   Narrative
7   On/Off Site
8   Insertion

Reprogramming

The process of creating inhabitable space in environments that were never intended to be used for those purposes can create a tension between old and new interiors and buildings. Reprogrammed space explores the tension between the requirements of the occupant and the environment in which the new interior is contained. This strategy can often be used to recolonize spaces that may have had a difficult or odious past, such as an abattoir becomes housing, or a politically and

ideologically "occupied" building is reused in a way that negates its own history. The reprogramming of space can afford the designer the opportunity to edit the past space in a way that they see fit to do so.

Intervention

Intervention is a strategy that involves the robust and often brutal imposition of the new into the old. Intervention creates a harmonious interior and one where new and old are integrated, yet clearly still distinct. It is a strategy that promotes continuity and quite often relies upon the careful and considered joining and detailing of specific materials. It can result in layered or palimpsest-like spaces. It can be a transgressive strategy that results in an interior that may feel imposed upon a space, creating an interior that feels like it shouldn't really be there.

Superuse

A phrase coined by 2012Architecten in Holland, Superuse involves the recycling of unusual material and its subsequent adaptation into a space. It is a strategy that has specific sustainable credentials and relates to the affordance of materials, objects, their durability and their value during lifetimes and patterns of consumption. Superuse has recycling and up-cycling connections; it uses found objects and thus can incorporate, sometimes wholesale, unusual elements being adapted and added to interior space, often in particular for their startling qualities.

Artifice

In the *Oxford English Dictionary*, the word *artifice* is described as the art of constructing, or the craft of the technician. It is also described as "an ingenious expedient, a maneuver, trick or device." In the dictionary of etymology, *artifice* is derived from the Latin word *artificium*, relating to "the employment of the art of cunning." Both descriptions suggest that artifice describes something that is crafted or assembled in order to create meanings, sometimes with the intention to deceive, seduce, or misinform its user. Interiors that are created using artifice can be designed to deceive, duplicate, or replicate the existing.

Installation

An installation is an "event-" based strategy that explores the extraction of drama and heightened contrast between the existing and the new. It incorporates the development of often non-site-specific installed spaces that are deemed temporal and often which are built not-to-last. Guerilla/pop-up, as well as event design along with distinct exhibitions and retail spaces are all designed to leave the existing as it was found once the interior is deemed out of fashion or the duration of the event is over.

Narrative

Environments that are designed to tell and enhance specific stories about spaces, objects, and their inhabitants can be derived from using a strategy that augments the existing spaces' storytelling potential. In contrast to new-build environments, existing spaces have a history, a past that can sometimes be utilized in the design of a new interior through having a story relayed or told. The strategy of enhancing and developing the narrative of an environment can lead to unique interior spaces.

On/Off Site

The construction and fabrication of elements both on- and off-site during a project is a strategy that leads to a variety of unusual interior solutions. Ready-made, specification, and bespoke fabrication can lead to the creation of specific and unique building reuse solutions. Quite often conservation, preservation, and restoration strategies are used in conjunction with this type of strategy in order to create an idealized backdrop for the placement of the new element.

Insertion

Insertion refers to the creation of interior space by using a strategy that promotes the placement of elements that are built-to-fit. An inserted interior suggests a process of putting it inside, in-between, on top of, around, upon, and under an existing space. The host space will often dictate the form and size of the new insertion but the new element(s) will be deliberately designed to contrast with the environment in which they are placed.

The reprocessing and re-editing of what is already extant could be considered to be a dominant form of cultural production. It has significant implications when considered as a method of designing the built

Medialab-Prado
At night the light and dynamic form of the Medialab-Prado is counterpointed by the concrete frame of the existing building.

Red Bull Academy
The temporary timber pavilions of
the academy are arranged around the
cast iron frame structure of the old
buildings of the abattoir.

environment in a world of finite resources.
The sustainable dimension of this approach
is made explicit in a number of the adaptive
strategies, but while it is not the primary
focus of this book, it assumes that this
emphasis is implicit. This book focuses on
the construction of new environments
from that which already exist in order to
substantiate the discipline of interiors. It
offers a unique addition to the growing
number of publications in this field and, it is
hoped, that while not a "manual" or "how
to" book on processes, its focus is on a
series of unique strategies for the creation
of the interior using key exemplars from
the recent history of the subject.

Notes

1   Christian Schittich. *Building in Existing Fabric:
    Refurbishment, Extension, New Design* (Basel:
    Birkhauser, 2004), 11.

2   Liz Diller of Diller & Scofidio & Renfro.
    Interviewed in *Surface Magazine*, 113 (November
    2014), 128.

3   "The Language of Conversion, the Conversion
    of Language." In *Reduce, Reuse, Recycle*, edited by
    Muck Petzet and Florian Heilmayer, 203. (Hatje
    Cantz Verlag, 2012).

4   Note to readers, throughout this book what is a
    first floor in the US and many parts of Europe, is
    considered the ground floor in the UK.

I
REPROGRAMMING

REPROGRAMMING INTRODUCTION

"Artists today program forms more than they compose them: rather than transfigure a raw element (blank canvas, clay etc.), they remix available forms and make use of data. In a universe of products for sale, preexisting forms, signals already emitted, buildings already constructed, paths marked out by their predecessors, artists no longer consider the artistic field (and here one can add television, cinema or literature) a museum containing works that must be cited or 'surpassed' as the modernist ideology of originality would have it, but so many storehouses filled with tools that should be used, stockpiles of data to manipulate and present."[1]

REPROGRAMMING

Reprogramming refers to using an item again, whether an object, edifice, or an idea, that has been repurposed with a new use. It is a deliberate and selective process in which the elements are withdrawn from their current context and placed into a new one, often in a way for which they were never originally intended. Reprogramming matter, objects, or edifices for new uses requires a thorough analysis of the qualities or features of the existing element that is to be redesignated. These qualities or features may or may not form part of the reprogramming, but an understanding of their meaning, in some form or other, is required nonetheless. According to Nicolas Bourriaud, the process of creating new works of art with matter and environments that were never intended to be used for those purposes has become the primary impulse for creativity in the twenty-first century.[2]

In the design of a new interior the strategy of reprogramming places great emphasis on use and occupancy. In other words, this approach stresses the importance of and, in some cases, the tension between the particular requirements and needs of the new occupants and the environment in which the new interior is to be contained. In particular, this process can create a tension between the old and new elements of the project, as the building envelope and its surrounding environment are analyzed and then adapted to host the new occupancy.

Reprogramming is an approach that can be used when a building no longer fits its purpose. It is a strategy that can be used to recolonize spaces that may have had a difficult or unusual past.

There are many reasons—economic, cultural, social, and more—that a building's previous use may be considered obnoxious or repulsive. An ideologically subjugated or dominated building with a disagreeable political history or an unpleasant previous use, such as a toxic factory or an abattoir, can be reused in a way that negates its own history. However, when a new interior is created inside the extant building, reprogramming ensures that there is a disruption between the old and the new. This break is one that separates the building's past use from its present and future use.

Whatever a building's reprogrammed use may be, the economic, cultural, and social conditions are all factors the designer of the new space may wish to consider when making the new interior space.

House of Air.
An old aircraft hangar has been adapted in order to house a new trampoline park. Part of the process of changing its use was its thorough decontamination, as it was covered in toxic lead paint and aviation fuel.

THE CITY OF THE BOOKS

PROJECT

THE CITY OF THE BOOKS

DESIGNERS

TALLER 6A

LOCATION

MEXICO CITY, MEXICO

DATE

2012

"The act of listening makes the building and agent in its own reinvention. . . . It is an exercise in full immersion, in as much the same way as language is learnt—it can be an uncontrolled affair, one of hearing a multitude of voices and making judgments about which make sense, which have a comprehensible syntax, and which are just noise."[3]

Buildings can outlast civilizations. Each successive generation may leave traces of its existence on the fabric of the buildings that it used. When designers reprogram a building, they may choose whether or not to account for the previous lives of the building. It is up to the designers of a building that is to be adapted to decide how important are the stories and echoes from the past. They can be listened to or disregarded.

La Ciudadela occupies a 7-acre plot of land in the center of Mexico City. It is a building with a long and ever-changing history. Conceived as the Royal Tobacco Factory, it was commissioned by the Spanish Crown at the beginning of the eighteenth century. In order to countenance its position on swampland, the immensely thick walls of the one-story building were constructed upon huge vaulted foundations. The four large courtyards of the building were used for drying leaves. The building became the "Citadel" in 1885 when its use was changed to that of a military post. At that time it became the city's arsenal, and later the northern barracks of the city garrison. Its use changed throughout the twentieth century; at various times it was a prison, a school, and a hospice for the poor. However, from 1946 until the present it has been a library. Before the 2010 reprograming, the last

1 The one-story building was constructed upon huge vaulted foundations to stop it from moving in the swamp in which it was built. The courtyard roofs were designed to be light, like umbrellas rising from the deep unstable marshes.

1

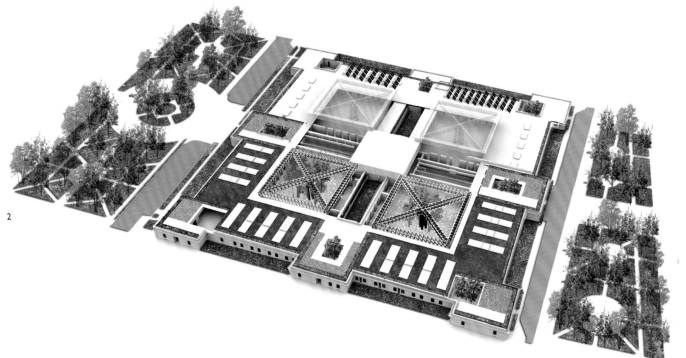

2

2 The master plan reinstated the
direct axial organization of the building
and connected the building back
to the city with newly landscaped
surroundings.

3 The Alejandro Rossi bookstore
is the first space entered on axis
from the main entrance. The five key
Mexican libraries are to the left in the
northwest wing of the building.

2—Bookstore
5–8—Courtyards
10–15—Five key Mexican libraries

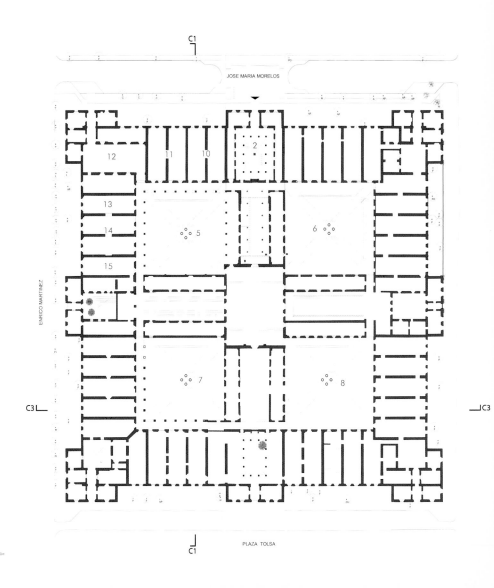

3

4 The bookstore was conceived as a giant bookcase that wraps the visitor in a floor-to-ceiling display of knowledge.

5 The covered courtyards allow library users to break out from the library stacks and sit and contemplate the changing uses of the existing building.

6 Distinctive features such as lighting elements are framed by the axial routes through the building.

4

significant change to the building took place in 1987 when the architect Abraham Zabludovsky enclosed the four courtyards with huge steel canopies, creating enclosed reading rooms for the library.

In 2010, Taller 6A was commissioned to revitalize the building and create a new master plan for the 325,000 square foot structure. The designers conceptualized the new project as the "City of the Books," reinventing the previous life of the building and updating its use to become a *citadel* of knowledge and a center for culture. Part of the project involved showcasing the intellectual journeys of five key Mexican thinkers through the housing of their own personal libraries within the walls of the building. Different teams of designers were appointed to design five spaces in the northwest wing of the library for the book collections of Ali Chumacero, Carlos Monsivais, Jose Luis Martinez, Jaime Garcia Terres, and Antonio Castro Leal.

5

Taller 6A concentrated on returning the building back to its former impressive conditions. The building was initially conceived as an efficient set of routes, with its own logic, first for the processing of tobacco, then for soldiers. Taller 6A set out to make the large building more efficient by reinstating the direct axial routes through the geometric interior. They did this by reorganizing the original patios and restoring the pathways that cross from north to south and in the perimeter of the building. Finally, they wanted to improve the environmental performance of the building by increasing natural light and ventilation as well as ensuring it complied with all the legislation regarding accessibility.

The regeneration of the library was symbolized by the Alejandro Rossi bookstore. Placed at the entrance to the building, the bookstore was designed not only to sell books but also to act as an exhibition space and introduction to the new city of knowledge. The long and narrow space was treated as an overscaled bookcase covering the walls and the floor. The deep recesses of the case contain books, screens, and seating. In the ceiling, the bookcase contains services such as lighting and air movement.

6

DESIGN REPUBLIC COMMUNE

PROJECT
DESIGN REPUBLIC
COMMUNE
DESIGNERS
NERI & HU DESIGN +
RESEARCH OFFICE (NHDRO)
LOCATION
SHANGHAI, CHINA
DATE
2012

"Buildings are fixed entities in the minds of most—the notion of the mutable space is virtually taboo—even in one's own house. People live in their space with temerity that is frightening. Homeowners generally do little more than maintain their property. It's baffling how rarely the people get involved in fundamentally changing their place by simply undoing it."[4]

When reprogramming an existing building with a new use, deleting certain elements of an interior can be a useful approach to creating order and coherence in a space. In order to articulate a new interior space, the subtraction and deletion of parts of an existing building can sometimes be as important as the addition of new elements. This can be described as the act of "undoing" a building, fundamentally changing a place not necessarily through the addition of new elements, but instead clarifying its meaning by emptying it of added accretions.

NHDRO designed the Design Republic Commune, a gathering space for designers and design patrons to enjoy and explore all aspects of design. It houses Design Republic, a contemporary furniture retailer, alongside a mixture of retail spaces that display and sell books, fashion, lighting, accessories, and flowers. The commune also contains a design gallery, an event space, a café, a restaurant with Michelin-starred Chef Jason Atherton, a one-bedroom apartment, as well as a satellite office for NHDRO.

3

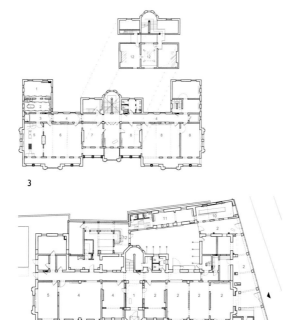

1

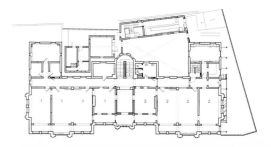

2

4

1 First-floor plan.
  1—Lobby
  2—Design republic
  4—Retail
  5—Bookstore
  10–12—Dining

2 Second-floor plan.
  1—Retail
  2—Design republic

3 Third-floor plan.
  1–7—Apartment
  8—Gallery
  12—Office

4 The glass-fronted showroom on the eastern side of the building is built upon the outlines of where the old storefronts once existed.

The host building, a police station constructed by the British in 1910, had changed use many times, most recently hosting an elementary school. Over the years, the changes to the building ensured that layers of alterations and adaptations had made the interior cluttered and incoherent. Realizing that not all of the changes were bad, and that some of the layers of change contained the stories of the building's history, NHDRO set about analyzing and taking stock of the many changes. They decided to retain some of the features that resulted from changes while eliminating others; removing unwanted elements with a series of strategic cuts and changes designed to enhance and clarify the fabric of the building. Where layers of previous uses had significantly accrued, the designers left them in situ, occasionally even framing them in glass to ensure they were represented for the next stages of the life of the building. Other parts of the building were radically altered. To impose a more ordered sequence of circulation the designers removed floors and walls to facilitate views through the rooms of the building akin to ensuring a flow through the spaces from room to room like a museum. The most significant addition was a new glass façade on the eastern, street side of the building. This replaced a series of illegally erected storefronts. The designers convinced the planning authorities to have them removed and then their outlines reinstated with a new transparent façade and a rooftop terrace extension.

5

5 Areas where significant layers of adaptations were revealed have been enclosed in glass and framed in order to preserve the past life of the building.

6 Removing the second floor lobby resulted in a new two-story entrance. The sleek, white box and frameless glass openings contrast with the clean red brick of the existing building.

Contrasting with the exterior, which was mostly left intact due to historic preservation requirements, the interior has been completely transformed. The starkly modern white rooms are juxtaposed with untouched remnants of brick walls and, in some cases, exposed wood lath underneath crumbling plaster walls. The clear and distinct detailing of the connections between the old and the new has created a visual and spatial tectonic balance between new and old elements in the reprogrammed building.

MISSOURI BANK

PROJECT

MISSOURI BANK:

CROSSROADS ARTS DISTRICT

DESIGNERS

HELIX ARCHITECTURE +

DESIGN

LOCATION

KANSAS CITY, USA

DATE

2008

"Re-use is not imitation and therefore not concerned with creating forgeries. It is a creative combination of old and new elements, which aims to re-elaborate, improve and carry further an idea, a style, an institution or a concept."[5]

Reprogramming an existing element, such as an object or a space, involves the remixing of what is already available, as opposed to the starting of a new element from scratch. Rather than the transformation of a new *blank canvas*, the designer is required to recompose what is already extant. This strategy of adaptation often includes the incorporation of elements of the existing material that is to be recomposed. It is a process that forms a new *composite construct* of material and space.

When he commissioned Helix to design two new bank branches and its new headquarters, Grant Burcham the CEO and president of Missouri Bank primed the designers with a brief stating that restoring customer's faith in a post-crash banking system was of paramount importance. Many of the existing customers were artists, gallery owners, and independent creative people: clients that were often overlooked by more mainstream banks. Therefore the new bank spaces needed to reflect and encourage the continuation of that diversity. Burcham wanted the new banks to avoid the clichés of normal financial spaces, with the separation of staff and customers through bulletproof glass. Instead, he stated, "Pretty much if someone said, 'that's what banks do,' we said, 'we don't want to do that.'"[6]

I

1 Dominated by two huge billboards, the existing mundane roadside building was previously an auto repair garage.

2 The open-plan banking hall is accessed via the main entrance from Southwest Boulevard. Customers can quickly utilize the bank's facilities via the drive-through window.

SOUTHWEST BOULEVARD

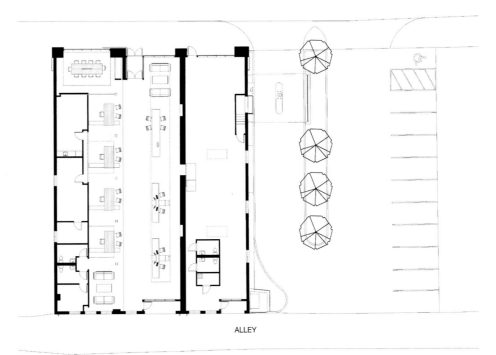

ALLEY

2

In keeping with this unusual approach to designing a financial institution, Burcham chose a 1920s former auto repair shop to house one of the new banks. Right in the middle of an emerging arts district in central Kansas City, Missouri, the area was full of warehouses and industrial buildings and spaces where their clientele were already working and living. The old one-story auto repair garage offered a very particular characterful space. It had a large, open plan interior in which to order the new bank space and it contained plenty of external parking spaces, where the cars were once lined up ready to be fixed.

The designers reprogrammed the garage space retaining many of its original features. The flat roof of the garage was greened and seeded for planting. The existing roof monitor lights were retained and refurbished. The long linear skylight, running the length of the building, provided natural daylight to the main banking hall below. The large garage doors were removed and were reglazed. Even the busy, drive-in aspect of the old repair shop was evoked through the placement of a drive through ATM attached to the side of the bank. Helix maintained a close connection to the previous use of the building.

The main entrance into the banking hall was positioned at the Southwest Boulevard side of the building. Once inside the space, a series of tellers positioned behind open desks greeted the customers. Accessible workstations are positioned to the side of the hall with more private spaces, such as bathrooms and staff rooms, located within the old staff spaces of the garage.

Early on in the design process Helix realized that the unusual site and clientele was reflected in the employees of the bank. During consultation the employees had asked for the new space to be like 'a farmers market, a café' or 'an art bus.' Helix realized the need to also include the work of the creative clients of the bank in the design process. Many of the artist clients were invited to work on the build itself and helped to source materials such as the salvaged pine boards from a local barn for the floor, and timber from the holding tanks of a defunct Kansas City vinegar factory. Even the billboards that towered over the mechanics workshop for years, and were considered part of the urban fabric, were retained. They are now used as "art boards," and local artists are chosen to exhibit their work in a highly visible, changing three-month external gallery space.

The success of the bank is down to the close connection between the client base, the owners and designers of the space and their understanding of the reprogramming of the existing building in which to house this new project.

3 The billboards announce the work of local artists to passersby in an ever-changing external urban gallery.

HOUSE OF AIR

PROJECT
HOUSE OF AIR
DESIGNERS
**MARK HORTON
ARCHITECTURE**
LOCATION
SAN FRANCISCO, USA
DATE
2011

"Adaptation is derived from the Latin *ad* (to) and *aptare* (fit). . . . It is taken to include any work to a building over and above maintenance to change its capacity, function or performance."[7]

Reprogramming existing buildings is a strategy that can sometimes involve the recolonization of spaces with an unusual or odious past. Buildings that were once used for a dirty or an unpleasant function, spaces that were once ideologically *occupied*, or buildings that were toxic or polluted from their previous function, often provide complex problems for the designers of the new use to solve. These types of projects often involve the remediation and extensive reworking of the fabric of the building to remove the effluents and toxins as well as the memories of the past, before the new use can be accommodated safely within the space.

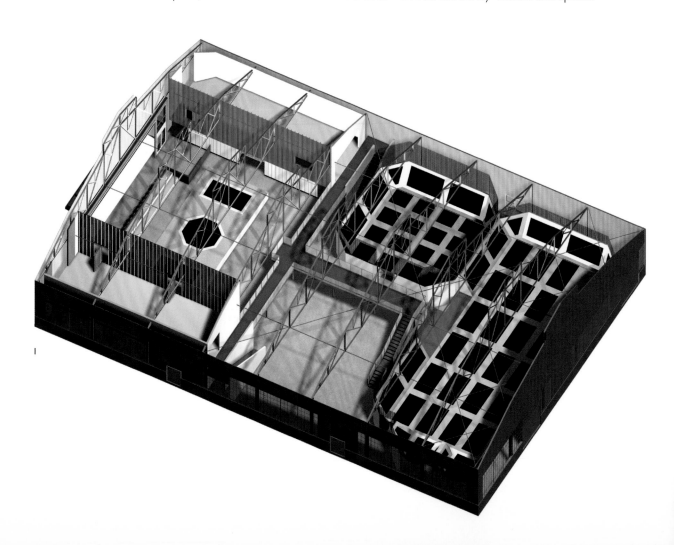

1

2   3

1 The single span structure of the hangar ensures that the large open spaces of the training field, dodge ball court, and the trampoline field are unencumbered by internal structures such as columns.

2 Building 926 at the foot of the image in the picturesque location of the airfield with views across the bay.

3 The listed exterior of the hangar was modified with a large picture of the building in its original use above the addition of a new bifold glass door.

In the shadow of the Golden Gate Bridge the Presidio military base had existed as a fortress since 1776. Its unusual location and short unsuitable airfield ultimately rendered it obsolete, and in 1994 it was decommissioned as a military zone to become the Golden Gate Recreational Park. Because of its illustrious aviation history, Building 926, one of a number of large aircraft hangars and support buildings on the site, was listed as a national monument. This severely restricted any radical external modifications to the building. Mark Horton Architecture had previously proposed an aviation museum on the site, a project that brought him to the attention of the owners of the "House of Air"; two entrepreneurs who wanted to convert the 1921 hangar into a place for a different type of flying—a trampoline park. The reprogramming of the hangar meant that it would form part of a new sports district, where a swimming pool, bike shop, and a rock-climbing gym would occupy other adjacent listed airfield buildings.

The existing building needed extensive modifications in order to allow it to be inhabited as a public building. The hangar was a lightweight steel structure sitting on natural landfill site prone to seismic activity. In order to be used as part of the public realm the building needed significant structural bracing and upgrading. The roof was very unusual in that it was a 6-inch (15-centimeter) thick solid concrete bombproof structure. This had to be restructured in order to comply with updated building regulations and to be kept in place during any possible seismic shaking. In addition to stabilizing the structure the building was considered a hazard due to pollution. The ninety year-old airplane hangar was covered in lead paint and aviation fuel, and it was riddled with asbestos. All of these complex issues had to be addressed before the building could be reused as a public space, a set of remedial works that would cost a sizeable portion of the allotted project budget.

4

As well as the works to the existing the hangar was reprogrammed with the addition of a series of significant elements. The listed exterior was modified with the addition of a huge 45-foot (15-meter) wide bifold glass plane that replaced the existing sliding hangar door. In good weather the door can be opened right out in order to frame the spectacular views of the park and the bay. In the front of the interior of the hangar are three performance trampolines, known as the training ground and used for both competitive jumping as well as ski, snowboard, and wakeboard training. Deeper into the hangar is a large field trampoline and a dodge ball court. Flanking the trampoline areas are two pavilions housing a café, meeting facilities, lockers, and a lounge. The pavilions are two stories and at the upper level of the full height of the hangar a lounge and party room, as well as their catwalk access, offer overviews of the lively action on the floors below.

The search for a suitable material identity, with which to enhance the highly animated interior, resulted in the designers opting for a simple language of off-the-peg materials. Translucent blue polycarbonate sheeting is used to clad the upper levels of the pavilions. Vertically orientated fluorescent tube lighting is sandwiched in the layers of the wall construction. Simple and cheap, they give the interior a cool-blue glow while their skyward orientation urges the trampolinists to go higher and higher.

5

4 The front of the interior of the project is animated by the "training ground," which consists of three performance trampolines.

5 Random openings in the blue polycarbonate cladding afford the visitor framed views down onto the lively lower floors of the building.

6 Two-story-high pavilions utilize the height of the hangar and flank the performance trampolines. They enclose the party room, lounge, and offices.

6

WEAVE

PROJECT

WEAVE, WATERLOO COMMUNITY CENTRE

DESIGNERS

COLLINS AND TURNER

LOCATION

SYDNEY, AUSTRALIA

DATE

2013

"Any given programme can be analysed, dismantled, deconstructed according to any rule or criterion and then be reconstructed into another programmatic configuration."[8]

Reprogramming is an approach that can be used when an existing building is no longer fit for purpose. It is a strategy that can be utilized in order to adapt a building in order to facilitate the same use but in a different way. This may be when its occupants have outgrown it, it may no longer work for what it was intended for, or the building may be just unappealing to its users and the community surrounding it.

Weave is a community service providing a range of services to disadvantaged young people. For over fifteen years Weave has been based in a converted amenities block overlooking the skate park at Waterloo Oval—an inner-city suburb of Sydney. The existing building was an uninviting, undynamic, one-story structure that appeared extraneous to the park and unwelcoming to its users. Through enhancing the relationship between the building, the landscape of the park, and the adjacent skate ramps and their users, the designers dramatically transformed the buildings dynamism, increasing its openness and re-emphasising its connection to the local community.

Through its reprogramming the building has been transformed into a welcoming counselling facility and communal workspace for Weave.

1

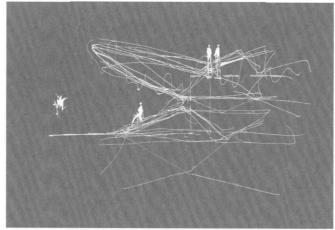

2

3

I   Before reprogramming, the
uninviting one-story amenities block
was unwelcoming and represented a
barrier to community interaction.

2   The concept sketch demonstrates
the intended enhanced relationship
between the landscape, building,
community, and the skate park users.

3   In time, the raw qualities of the
mesh and steel canopy will be offset
by the plants and flowers that cover it
as it "disappears" into the park.

The main transformation of the building involved the opening out of the previously
solid walled structure and increasing its presence in the park. This has been
achieved through the application of a dynamic steel mesh structure, forming a
canopy that wraps the building in a dramatic fashion. The canopy was fabricated
from galvanized steel structural sections with additional mesh panels, evoking the
language of familiar urban elements such as railings, crash barriers, shutters, and
gratings in the landscape of the inner city. The canopy contains a landscaped roof
garden. It has been designed to support a variety of native climbing and fruiting
plants. In plan the canopy is star shaped and each point marks a new opening, such
as the door or newly constructed bay window areas, in the four corners of the
existing building.

With this addition, the reprogrammed building has become an extension of its
landscape setting, combining architecture and horticulture in a unique way. The
new sculptural form now enlivens the southern area of the Waterloo site.
As the plants mature and grow across the canopy, the building will gradually merge
with its park setting, becoming an abstract and sculptural green landform that
punctuates the park boundary and visually merges with the adjacent tree canopies.

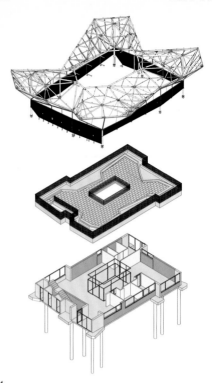

4

5

4 The addition of the canopy and external screens has radically altered the mundane amenities block that Weave once inhabited.

5 The courtyard both cools and lights the office spaces. Wooden floors and walls graffiti'd by the skaters offset the unfinished concrete soffit.

6 The central courtyard dominates the organization of the interior. The new dynamic mesh wrap offsets the orthogonal geometry of the existing building.

The interior is arranged around a new central courtyard. The building contains a reception area, two counselling rooms, a relaxing room, manager's office, kitchenette, and a small facility for a visiting general practitioner. The interior is open and flexible and now has workspaces for fourteen staff. Internally, materials are paired back and simply detailed. The retained existing brick walls are white-washed, and contrasted against raw expressive concrete soffits and new structural columns. The rooftop and courtyard plants are visible from many of the interior spaces, reinforcing the connection of the building to the park.

The building was designed to be robust, low maintenance, and long lasting with a low environmental impact with minimal energy costs. Internally, conditions are passively controlled using natural cross ventilation, exposed thermal mass, and a building envelope shaded by the canopy structure and climbing plants. The new courtyard brings daylight and fresh air into the depths of the building, minimizing reliance on artificial lighting and negating the need for air conditioning.

The designers have also considered the next chapter of the possible reprogramming of the building. If Weave were ever to move on, the interlocking but self-supported steel canopy structure can be demounted and relocated to a different place.

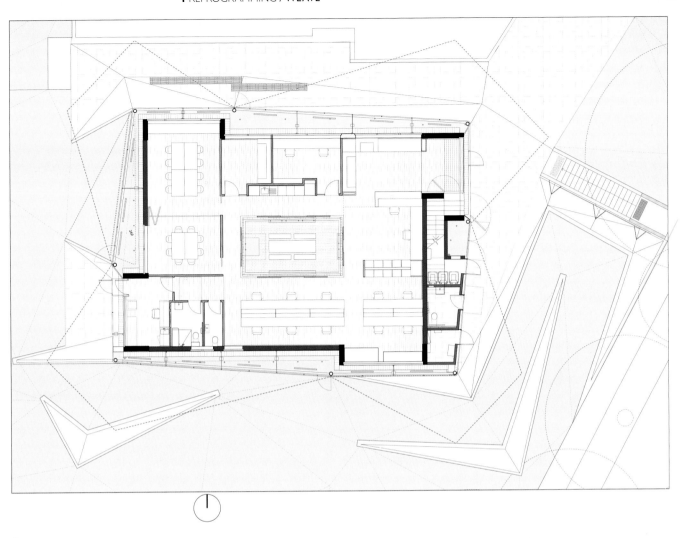

6

Notes

1. Nicolas Bourriaud, *Postproduction* (New York: Lukas & Steinberg, 2002), 17.

2. Ibid.

3. David Littlefield and Saskia Lewis, *Architectural Voices: Listening to Old Buildings* (London: Wiley-Academy, 2007), 10.

4. Peter Muir, *Gordon Matta-Clark's Conical Intersect: Sculpture, Space, and the Cultural Value of Urban Imagery* (Surrey: Ashgate, 2014), 61.

5. Julia Hegewald and Subrata Mitra, *Re-Use—The Art and Politics of Integration and Anxiety* (London: Sage, 2012), 48.

6. Grant Burcham, "Missouri Bank Branches," *Architect* (2012), 107, retrieved from http://www.architectmagazine.com.

7. James Douglas, *Building Adaptation* (Oxford: Butterworth Heinemann, 2006), 1.

8. Bernard Tschumi, *Questions of Space* (London: AA Publications, 1990), 104.

2
INTERVENTION

INTERVENTION INTRODUCTION

"Enabling work equally rises from the regions of the pragmatic in conventional building to the level of thoughtful strategy in works of intervention. Whereas in straightforward architectural work the site must be readied for the footings of a new building, existing structures demolished, the ground stabilized sometimes by draining a pond or suchlike, work that needs the least instruction for the builder, with intervention such work requires a surgical precision. The partial demolitions of and removals from the host building are in one sense like a shadow being cast of the new work to come."[1]

Described in the *Oxford English Dictionary* as "to happen or to take place in between," *intervention* is a strategy that can integrate the existing building with the elements of the new use but always in a very distinct and clear way. It is a strategy that involves the robust and often brutal imposition of the new into the old yet with a subtlety that creates a harmonious space and one where both are often integrated. Intervention is a strategy where the act of stepping in-between the existing building and the new use and affecting the way in which the next courses of action are to be undertaken, always within the context that this work may well be just one more alteration in a series of further changes to come.

As Fred Scott suggests, an interventionist approach can result in surgical like methodology or process, one that may involve repair and/or selective demolition, in order to create a suitable and appropriate basis for the intervention. Yet the new work will have a close relationship to the old, with the existing building often offering a set of oblique guidelines for the designer of the intervention to translate as to how the extant space may be reused.

Because of its robust tendencies, intervention is often used to stabilize or act as an armature for buildings that are ruined and even on the point of collapse. Intervention then becomes a process of negotiation between what is to be stabilized and what is to be pulled down. It is, in effect, a way of editing extant structures in a way that can be restorative and also narrative. It does this in the way that it will intercede between different accounts of what is and was once there and what is about to be. Because of its surgical like qualities, it can be an expedient and pragmatic way of clarifying and articulating spaces that might be considered incoherent, and through multiple changes of use need to be clarified and ordered. In this instance intervention is more subtractive, editing a building in order to return a space back to some form of clarity and purpose. An intervention approach to a new interior will ensure that the new and the old elements of the space will be intertwined.

Finally, one of the key characteristics of intervention is that the disruption, or break, between the old building and the new elements is a crucial junction. It is a strategy that encourages connection and definition between the existing building and the new elements and yet it is quite often reliant upon the careful and considered joining and detailing of specific materials. In order for a successful intervention to be realized the disruption or break needs to be clearly defined and articulated. This is often managed by favoring a material confrontation, a distinctive connection between the extant material and something completely new. Because of this approach it is made clear that intervention does not imitate and replicate; it is a creative combination of old and new elements that aims to advance the existing building through new forms of occupation.

Astley Castle
The old crumbling ruin of the castle building was rescued and restructured with a new armature masonry structure that reinforced and stabilized the existing building.

YOHJI YAMAMOTO

PROJECT

YOHJI YAMAMOTO

DESIGNERS

JUNYA ISHIGAMI ASSOCIATES

LOCATION

NEW YORK CITY, USA

DATE

2008

"'The work of intervention is therefore based on an analysis, of thought that must be both intelligent and intuitive. The work of intervention then proceeds, founded upon this initial analysis."[2]

Throughout the lifetime of a building, the addition and subtraction of elements to its fabric can ensure that it becomes unrecognizable. Sometimes this renders it no longer fit for its purpose. When understanding the history of these changes, and with a desire to return the building back to some semblance of coherence, a simple intervention into an existing space can provide an expedient and pragmatic way of clarifying a space. Through analysis and then response, intervention can be an instrument to be used for implementing radical changes and ultimately some form of coherence upon an existing building.

A single-story brick building in the meatpacking district of New York City occupies the tip of a two-street intersection at the confluence of Gansevoort and West 13th Street. Over fifty years ago the Y-junction site was filled to its perimeter by a simple, brick factory building with large windows. Subsequently, the building changed use many times until in 2007 when it became empty and abandoned. Yohji Yamamoto commissioned Junya Ishigami to construct a new flagship store in the simple, yet, unusually shaped building. Open on three sides, and with visitors arriving from all aspects of the building, Ishigami decided to intervene into the building with two strategic cuts, one to create a new opening and entrance and one to heighten the impact of the sharp end of the triangle. The opening cut dissected the building into two parts, forming a new alleyway through which visitors could enter the building. As well as controlling the point of entrance through this single cut, the building was bifurcated into two elements: a service space and the front of house. When required, staff could use the new entrance to drift between the showroom and then the stockroom. Another cut to the front of the building took the edge off the sharp front of the space and created what Ishigami described as a move that reduced "the strong sense of frontality at the front corner, which allowed each of the three elevations to feel like a front."[3] The brick outline of the previous sharp edge was outlined on the floor of Gansevoort Street as a reminder of the old building.

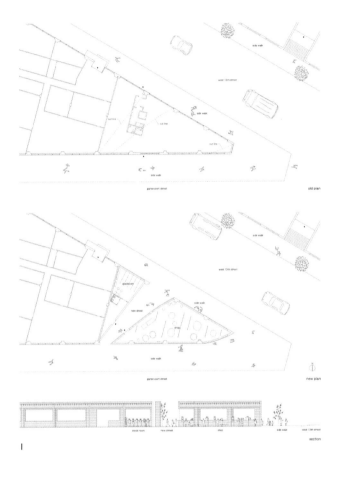

1

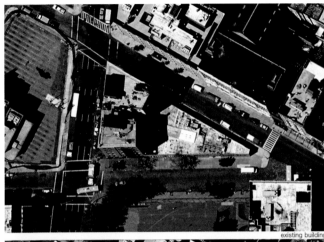

existing building

after cutting the building

2

1 Before and after the cuts. The smaller part of the building became the stockroom.

2 The unique location of the building at the confluence of two important streets directly influenced its form. Ishigami reacted to the building site by intervening into the building with a diagonal cut through the space and by rounding off its sharp, pointed end.

3

3 The interventions into the building echo the simplicity of the concept sketch.

4 The frameless, glass windows reinforce the balance between solid brick and transparency, while offering views through the space.

5 The new cut became a shortcut through the site as well as the focus for visitors, as it contains the new entrance for the store.

Through the creation of a new shortcut through the site the designer clarified the building's relationship to the street. This also allowed the building's program to be separated into two parts. This pragmatic approach clarified the interior of the space, separating server and serviced space. The gentle curve of the front end of the building redirected the sharp focus of the triangular shape, easing its dynamism and allowing it to be read from all three sides. The separation of the tip of the triangle was akin to setting the building free of its anchor, like a ship slipping from its moorings in the nearby Hudson River. The large windows of the building were reglazed to make a new distinctive façade, with views into and through the interior space. With two bold interventions the designer had clarified the building not only in its relation to the site but also as to how it would function as a retail space.

4

5

HOUSE SURGERY

PROJECT

HOUSE SURGERY

DESIGNERS

KATSUHIRO MIYAMOTO
& ATELIER CINQUIÉME
ARCHITECTS

LOCATION

TAKARZUKA-CITY, HYOGO,
JAPAN

DATE

1997

"I suppose that the loads will be gradually transferred to the steel framework. The wooden framework will retire from the structure, and then it will exist just as a fixture which retains the memory of the habitant's lives and the earthquake disaster."[4]

Sometimes an event takes place that changes a city and its urban infrastructure forever. In this context the choice of whether to retain or demolish is not always one that is taken by the designers of a new building. Instead structures may be considered unsafe or damaged beyond repair. Intervention can be used as a strategy that can assist the process of rebuilding the city through the retention and reuse of its existing buildings and spaces. It can also be utilized as an instrument that enables both new and old to coexist in order to narrate history and chart progress, especially in a difficult or distressing context.

The Hanshin-Awaji earthquake or Kobe earthquake of 1995 resulted in the loss of 6,300 lives. One of the hardest hit areas was the cities and suburbs of the Hyogo Prefecture. One in five homes were destroyed or rendered uninhabitable by the shock, and a quarter of public buildings were damaged beyond repair. Most of the buildings that were constructed after 1981 survived the earthquake, as they were built to a new set of codes that ensured they were shock resistant. However, buildings that were not constructed to those standards suffered serious structural damage or complete collapse. Many of the older traditional houses in the district had heavy tiled roofs that weighed around 2 tons. These were structured in order to resist the frequent typhoons that plagued Kobe and the surrounding areas. The roofs tended to be supported by a light timber structural frame only. In the earthquake, when the wood supports gave way in the tremors, the roofs collapsed the unreinforced walls and floors and flattened the houses, resulting in the loss of many lives.

1   The bracing and supporting effect of the steelwork is fully exposed in the long section.

2   A series of models were used to formulate the correct structural response and requirements to bring the building up to earthquake-resistant codes and standards.

3/4 The majority of the interior spaces are retained and left intact by the new structural interventions.

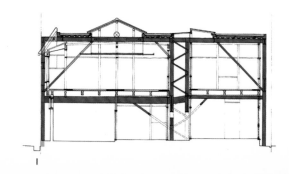

I

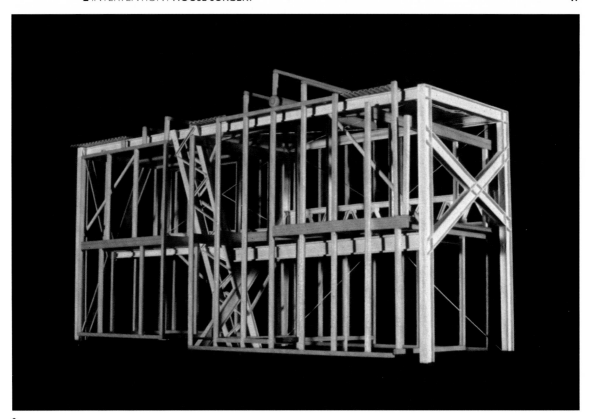

2

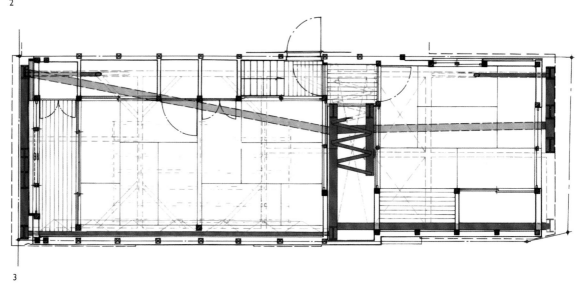

3

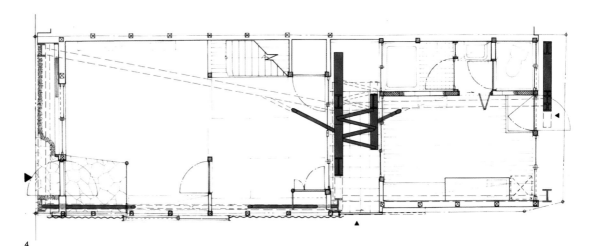

4

5

6

7

Constructed in the 1900s, the house that Katsuhiro Miyamoto was born in was so severely damaged in the disaster that the local authorities deemed the house uninhabitable. The sentimental value that Miyamoto felt for the building, the family memories, and the histories of the spaces, prompted a different response to the authorities' desire to demolish and start again. The designer did not want to forget the disaster by removing all signs of the tragedy. Instead he wanted the urban environment to remember and, in some way, reflect this tumultuous period in its recent history. Rather than lose the character of the site and demolish the terrace of houses in which his home sat, Miyamoto proposed to intervene upon the ruin with a new structure that would impact upon the existing building in such a way as to render it a hybrid of new and old structures and as a monument to the recent past. The new hybrid would serve the pragmatic function of bringing the terrace and the house up to current regulations and it would also act as a reminder of the earthquake.

Miyamoto chose to convert the building into an office for his practice by intervening into the existing wooden structure with a new steel frame. The frame would act as a support and brace for the old timber beams and columns. The designer likened this process to a patient in a hospital, wrapped in a plaster cast after an accident in which they have broken their limbs. The frame was designed to be a support not just for the existing building but it is also a metaphor for the healing of the house and the city after the disaster that befell it.

The frame was unceremoniously placed back amid the structure of the house. Then the wooden beams and columns were lashed to the new frame. The effect upon the interior ensures that the new intervention is clearly distinguished from the old and, in some places, its dynamic quality is enhanced by leaving the junctions between new and old left brutally exposed. The new structure is evident in each room, a constant reminder of the history of the city and the room.

BUNKER 599

PROJECT

BUNKER 599

DESIGNERS

RAAAF/ATELIER DE LYON

LOCATION

CULEMBORG, NETHERLANDS

DATE

2013

"Different local contexts produce different form of resistance. The strategies activists develop and the objects they make depend on the cultures they are a part of and the particular challenges they face. Activist makers work by any media necessary, from interventions on the ground to actions on the Internet."[5]

Intervention is a robust strategy that can quite often adapt an existing building in a brutal and, sometimes, a harsh manner. It is used when it is necessary to transform a building that may itself be robust, tough, and built to last. Sometimes intervention is to brutally transform something that is symbolic of an odious or difficult past. In whatever manner it is used, it will always result in a transformation of the existing building in order for it to mean something quite different from which it was originally constructed to contain.

Built as part of a 53-mile (85-kilometer) new Dutch waterline project, a line of water defenses, constructed in the seventeenth century to allow Holland to resist military invasion, Fort 599 was part of a series of 1940 additions of bunkers and pillboxes designed to keep out the German army. The New Dutch Waterline (NDW) was a line of military defense that protected the cities of Muiden, Utrecht, Vreeswijk, and Gorinchem. It was a form of defense that was intended to slow down any potential invasion by means of intentional flooding. Bypassed by German paratroopers in 1940, before any flooding could be enabled, the line of defense was abandoned after the war; yet, due to the impregnable construction of the buildings, the pillboxes and bunkers remained.

1 The bunker before intervention. The landscape around the structure was cleared to the waterline to make space for the new path.

2 The new path invites the visitor to pass through the monolithic bunker interior and onto a timber pier on the waterway.

1

As part of a central government master plan their historical importance was recognized and then developed as part of a plan for a new linear national park. From the year 2000 a twenty-year plan has been implemented to revitalize and reuse the military landscape. Other fortifications in the line have already been reused as cafes, hostels, and even a botanical garden. Bunker 599 was reused as a place to view the nature reserve as well as a place to reflect upon Dutch history and its relationship to its landscape.

The squat features and bulk of the reinforced concrete structure was adapted by reversing the relationship between its interior and exterior. This was achieved by cutting it open into two pieces. Split into two halves the designers repurposed the bunker into a sharply defined framing device for the waterway beyond. A new pathway leads visitors from the hill behind the bunker through the middle of the structure and then onto a timber jetty in the *Diefdijk* waterway. This sequence reverses the previously inaccessible nature of the bunker, instead opening it up and returning it to finally become an integral part of the landscape that it was originally designed to defend at all costs.

3 The aggregate of the concrete is exposed in the slice through the walls of the bunker.

4 As visitors descend from the hillside they are drawn toward the water.

3

5 The view to the waterway is sharply framed by the reinforced concrete walls of the structure.

6 The view back toward the hill from the jetty.

ASTLEY CASTLE

PROJECT
ASTLEY CASTLE
DESIGNERS
WITHERFORD WATSON
MANN
LOCATION
WARWICKSHIRE, UK
DATE
2012

"Current architectural practice in historic settings tends to be polarised between two positions:
- the studious repair or reconstruction of the historic building
- completely contrasting construction beside or within the historic building: as one critic put it, 'placing the past in inverted commas'

These positions share the belief that history is past. By contrast, we are convinced that history is not what happened to other people, but a dimension of human nature, and a fundamental part of our working conditions, even in the modern age."[6]

An intervention strategy can be used to rescue structures that are sometimes considered beyond repair. The intervention may take the form of a structural element, one that acts as an armature, reinforcing and stabilizing the existing building. This type of intervention may act as a mediator, performing not just as an arbitrator of structural requirements but it may also define enclosures and make particular rooms for certain types of occupation. The placement of such an intervention may require surgical-like precision, enforcing a procedure with which to mediate between what is already there and what is new.

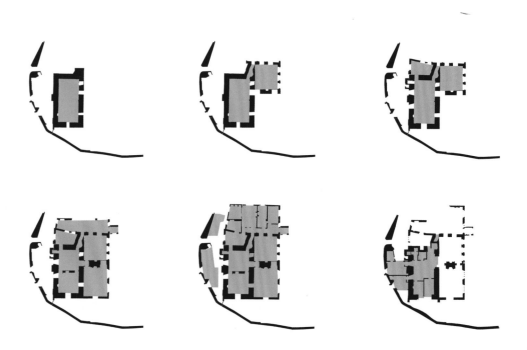

1 Top (L–R) Thirteenth century,
fifteenth century, early sixteenth
century
Bottom (L–R) Early seventeenth
century, early nineteenth century,
twenty-first century

2 Entrance through the courtyard
into the hall of the house. The
bedrooms are on this level, and the
main living space is reached via the
stairs.

2

Astley Castle has a long and interesting history that stretches back to its beginnings
on the current site in the eleventh century. Described as a castle, it is really a
fortified manor house that was crenellated and moated in 1266. The fortress house
has played a significant part in the history of Britain. Described as "the home of the
three queens of England," at various times it housed Elizabeth of York, the wife of
Henry VII, and Lady Jane Grey, who met an untimely end in 1554. The turbulent
history of the house culminated in 1978 when, currently in use as a hotel, a
mysterious fire gutted and ruined the building. Its Grade II listing belies the fact that
up until 2008 it was in an advanced state of decay and was facing total collapse as
vandalism and the stripping out of anything worth taking had reduced the building
to an unstable mess.

3

4

3 The distinction between the new intervention and the old ruins is evident even from a distance.

4 Floor to ceiling glazing at the upper level of the house frames dramatic views of the ruins and the landscape beyond.

5 The new brickwork embraces and supports the ancient chimney stack, which forms the backdrop to an open courtyard overlooked by the main living space.

6 The second-floor living space is located in the oldest part of the ruin and adopts the epic proportions of a medieval hall.

In a 2005 competition to recover the building, initiated by the Landmark Trust, a large number of entries proposed how the building could be stabilized and then reoccupied. The scale of the site and the extent of the damage made a traditional restoration project unfeasible. WWM won the competition with a proposal to make a house within the ruin, one that would not only consolidate the ruin but also make it a great space to rent and live in for holiday-length stays. Drawing on both the scale and complexity of the project, the history of the site influenced the design of an upside-down house, one that was placed into the thirteenth-century fragment of the building. The house would be inverted, with its bedrooms on the first floor and a large living, kitchen, and dining space on the upper level. Much like a medieval hall, the upper floor would be open and would connect the visitors with stunning views back across the landscape.

Early phases of the project involved clearing the collapsed material from the ruins and a forensic analysis of the existing building. The ruins were stabilized in a two-part procedure. First, there was a discreet stitching together of the existing walls with a series of invisible ties, ensuring a relatively stable shell. Then, a new armature of concrete and steel that formed the brace and the main structural frame for the new timber house was added. Carefully chosen bricks were used to build upon the ruined walls. These were thinner than regular bricks, and were chosen because they were able to accommodate the irregularities of the rough walls. Their contrast was important. The final layer of occupation was in the form of a timber construction for the house, creating a warm and inviting environment where the difference between new and old are evident and yet their complementary character is never forgotten.

5

6

TWIGGY

PROJECT
TWIGGY
DESIGNERS
ARCHITECTEN DE VYLDER
VINCK TAILLIEU BVBA
LOCATION
GHENT, BELGIUM
DATE
2012

"Ultimately, interiors are the receptacles of things, but also the support of affects. These things are not simply the objects that provide material support for memory. They are also commodities on display, on offer in the market."[7]

Using intervention as a strategy for the remodeling of existing buildings is an approach that is akin to editing things, affects, and spaces. It can be a method that enhances or suppresses the previous lives and uses of the space. The previous history of the building is a narrative that can be communicated like a story—a material account of the building. The designers of the latest addition plot how they may add to and ultimately finish the tale—for now.

Architecten de Vylder Vinck Taillieu were commissioned to create a new clothing store in a listed and protected eighteenth-century townhouse in the center of Ghent. One specific project requirement was to bring the historic monument up to current regulatory levels, particularly in circulation through the building and through egress in case of fire. The project had to include a new external stair that needed to be added across the back of the listed rear façade.

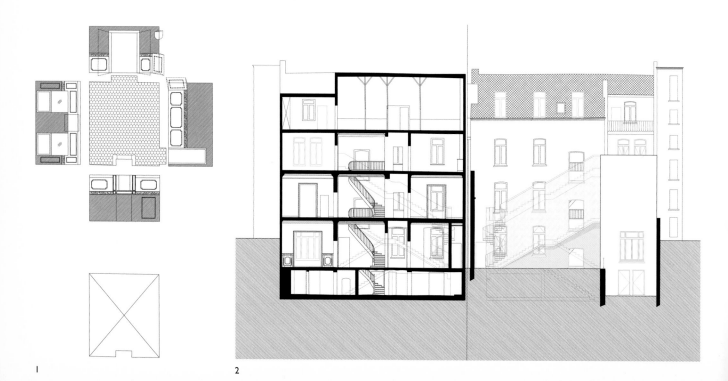

1

2

1 Each room was carefully analyzed and recorded through drawing in order to retain its character and identity through the processes of scraping away the existing surfaces.

2 The existing vertical circulation was preserved, and a new fire stair was added to the rear of the building. The new addition containing the stair replicated the back façade exactly, including its windows.

3 Fluorescent orange-red paint was used to highlight the doorways that were considered erratic additions to the existing building.

3

As well as the addition of a new rear stairwell, intervention was used as a strategy for the subtraction of elements of the building. As with many old buildings, the history of the space was a story of accretion. Over time, the addition of many new openings and, in particular, doorways into the various grand rooms of the building resulted in a certain level of spatial incoherence. Wishing to return some coherence to the interior, yet also wishing to highlight the changes in the building over time, Architecten de Vylder Vinck Taillieu removed many of the doors but left the openings, playfully painting them fluorescent orange-red in order to highlight their redundancy. As well as removing what were considered to be erratic additions, the designers scraped away the layers of wallpaper and paint found in each room. They then left the walls unfinished, creating a new surface for each room.

To reinforce the connections between shopper and display area to the basement display area the floor of the front ground room was removed. This created a two-story space viewable upon entrance through a secret wooden panel. The removal of the floor and the expression of unifying the space as a whole entity was then contrasted by the retention of the entire ornate wood paneling that lined both rooms. This included retaining the elegant marbled fireplaces attached to the upper and lower sections of the chimneystack. This opened the two-story space, yet reinforced its reading as two separate entities, and created a surreal atmosphere with a fireplace that visitors cannot reach.

The addition to the back of the building was equally as surreal. The new fire stair is housed in what appears to be a bulge in the back of the building. The designers replicated the existing façade, complete with windows, in a wedge that accommodated the new stair. To enhance the strange quality of the addition the interior was lined with mirrors.

Throughout the interior, views are enhanced through the opening of doorways, windows, and passages. Where possible, new lighting, trunking, and any associated pipe work is exposed, giving the impression of the work on the building being in progress. Among this backdrop, the clothes and shoes are stacked irreverently on crates and in boxes, as well as occasionally on a mannequin. The whole ensemble has the appearance of a work that still appears to be unfolding throughout the interior of the grand building.

4   5

4 Retaining the wood paneling and keeping the fireplaces one floating in the air heightened the surreal atmosphere of the new two-story space.

5 Each room derives its character from the found qualities of what appeared when the wallpaper and paint were scraped away. New lighting, cable, and pipe work were exposed, adding to the effect of a work in progress.

6 Removing the floor created a two-story space that reveals the basement which is viewed through an opening in the wood paneling that surrounds the room.

6

Notes

1. Fred Scott. *On Altering Architecture* (Abingdon Oxford, Routledge, 2008), 126.

2. Ibid, at 116.

3. Cited in "Renovation: Beyond Metabolism'"by Ralph Sobell. Japan Architect Yearbook, 2008, JA73 118.

4. Sent in an e-mail exchange with Katsuhiro Miyamoto and sent with pictures May 18, 2014.

5. Text taken from a display panel at the Disobedient Objects Exhibition. V+A Museum, London, Jan. 2015.

6. WWM Brochure sent accompanying work images, Aug. 27, 2014.

7. Georges Teyssot. *A Topology of Everyday Constellations* (Boston: MIT Press, 2013), 117.

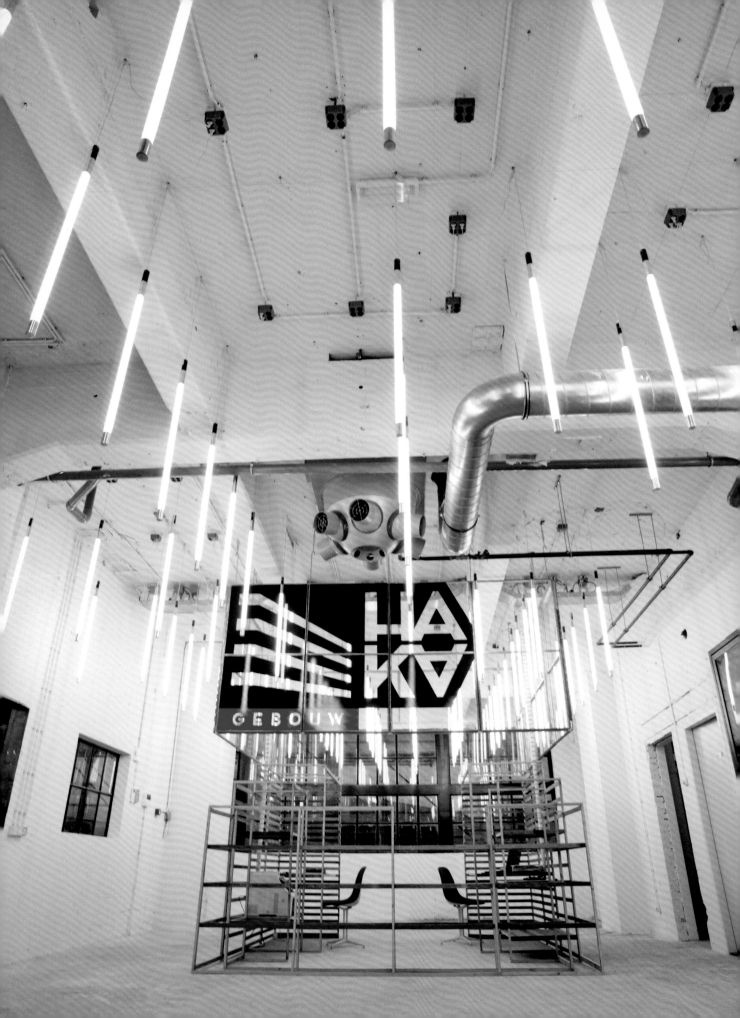

3
SUPERUSE

SUPERUSE INTRODUCTION

"In Superuse heaven, architects and builders would be able to get at least a share of the materials they need for the new building from the structure that would have been at the same spot."[1]

Superuse is a turn of phrase first coined by 2012Architecten, a group of designers and architects in Holland. They decided that ingenious, social design solutions could be created using existing resources, materials, and systems. The group is engaged with the reuse of waste and the opportunities inherent in being able to experiment with an overabundance of redundant materials. Superuse is a strategy that involves the recycling of waste and its incorporation into new objects and edifices. It is a strategy that has particular sustainable credentials and is an approach that is reliant on the affordance of materials, objects, their durability and their value as well as their modes of consumption. The strategy has recycling and up-cycling implications; it utilizes found objects and thus can incorporate, sometimes wholesale, unusual elements being adapted and added to interior space. In particular this is often undertaken for its startling qualities.

Superuse essentially denotes a process. It is one that the designers suggest can manifest itself in three main flows. One is the utilization of production waste. This includes reworking cut-offs, leftovers, and elements that cannot be recycled back into the flow of production. This includes things made as temporary objects to facilitate production but are often too large and valuable to just scrap. The second type of superuse process is the utilization of materials that can be withdrawn from their production process and reused in another context. This can include recycled elements and things sold and bought many times over, and products superseded through changes in regulation, such as car parts, washing machines, refrigerators, freezers, etc. This also includes materials that can be saved from scrapping. The third process of superuse is when a product has reached the end of its lifecycle. Old tires, car parts, and so on are all products that are often not recycled and end up in scrap yards or landfills.

The challenge in using a superuse strategy is to recognize how and when to use products and to be in control of the change of meaning that this approach to design obviously brings. 2012Architecten developed a strategy that they called the "Harvest Map." This involves developing a map around the site of the new construction from which one documents all possibilities of waste, by-products, and areas for salvage. These would then be harvested for their potential.

Any process that utilizes waste is reliant on contingency. Any sustainable approach to making an interior that uses waste can be applied to not only buildings but also elements that are a part of their production. This includes materials that might be found either inside or outside of the design and construction processes. Sometimes the production of these elements can be off-site, and the materials and elements can be produced away from the construction processes. Other times these processes of recycling can be made on-site. The reallocation of certain materials can be realized partly through contingencies; a surplus of materials can lead to their reuse partly due to the mere fact that waste needs to be redesignated. Whatever the reason for the redesignation of materials the aim of these options is to make the most of resources and cut down on the growth of landfills and waste.

HAKA Recycle Office
The auditorium was enclosed by a wall constructed from reclaimed clothing with the seating made from salvaged timber.

PALAIS DE TOKYO

PROJECT

PALAIS DE TOKYO

DESIGNERS

LACATON AND VASSAL

LOCATION

PARIS, FRANCE

DATE

2001/2012 (PHASE 1+2)

"We are much more interested in the principle of addition than in simply replacing what is there with something new. It isn't a question of 'one or the other' but a question of 'one and the other.' That's why what already exists, and what we find in place, no matter what its components may be, is always enrichment. That is much more important to us than simply building a form."[2]

Superuse is a strategy for constructing buildings from surplus materials. Abandoned buildings are leftovers that still have resonant meanings; they are spaces that can be reactivated and enriched through reuse in order to create distinct and unusual places.

Built in 1937 for the Paris Art and Technology World Expo, the Palais De Tokyo was conceived as a modern-art gallery for France and the city of Paris. Configured into two symmetric wings, connected by a central colonnade, its designers Dondel, Aubard, Viard, and Dastague conceived it in a monumental classical style. They realized the building with a brutal, reinforced concrete frame, clad in a stone finish. An epic stair, of monumental proportions, linked the gallery to the street and connected the colonnade to its riverside location.

While one wing has remained in use as the Musee d'art Moderne de la Ville, the western wing of the building was abandoned for many years. In 1999, a competition was held to design a new gallery with open, flexible space for temporary exhibitions and events.

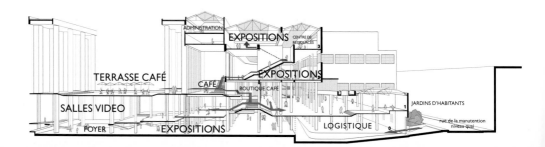

1

1 The flow of the gallery spaces within the building and their connection and overlap with each other can be seen in the sectional perspective.

2 The second-floor plan shows the organisation of the building.

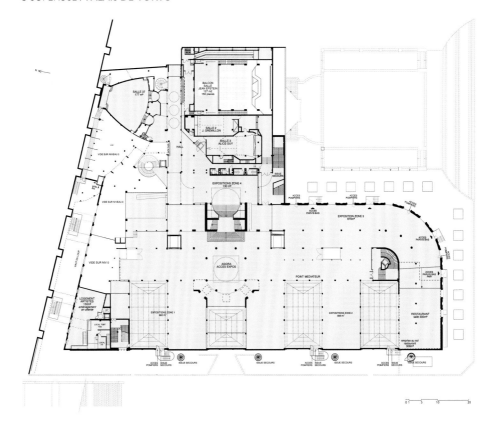

2

The designers Lacaton and Vassal won the first competition for the project. Constructed on a very small budget the designers approached the design of the building through the exploitation of the qualities of the existing spaces. The popularity of the project has meant that in 2001 the initial reworking of the 86,111 square feet (8,000 square meters) of the first phase has now been completed thirteen years later by the adaptation of the other 172,222 square feet (16,000 square meters). The second phase included more specific areas associated with a gallery, such as auditoriums, a concert hall, a restaurant, a bookstore, and offices.

The site had been stripped out ten years before work began in an aborted attempt to convert it into the Palais Du Cinema. Lacaton and Vassal found the building in a condition where they decided to demolish nothing. Instead they would be as efficient as possible with the existing structure. Remaindered elements of the previous stripping out were either left as found or, if needed, repaired and improved to meet contemporary regulatory standards. Meeting these standards meant that the testing of the stripped out concrete frame ensured that the exposed reinforced steel bars in the structure had to be checked for adequate protection. The designers wanted to resist spray-on fireproofing so they simulated fires against the structure with which to convince the authorities that the building's raw state could handle any adverse conditions.

The processes of the first phase were undertaken with one eye on the second phase of work. This meant that years later the designers reworked their own initial designs via an incremental approach to the existing building.

3 The exposed, concrete frame of the building was left in a raw condition, subject to adequate tests that included setting fires against it.

4 The existing building is occupied in order to form a series of galleries where a variety of events and exhibitions can take place.

5 The stripped out building was left as found and only repaired where necessary to meet regulatory requirements.

6 Second phase works included the addition of elements such as a bookstore.

Entering through the colonnade, the monumental interior landscape is read as a series of unfinished terrains upon which occupancy, in the form of art works and their observers, unfolds. The found quality of the interior manifests itself as a series of undisturbed spaces with peeling paintwork surfaces. Left over signage and indentations evoke the ghosts of previous occupants and their activities.

The monumentality of the building was complemented with the implementation of a natural lighting strategy that manifested itself as roof lights, and large floor-to-ceiling windows on the principal façades of the building. The desire to convert the building to a cinema meant these openings were once covered up. Lacaton and Vassal repaired and waterproofed the roof lights and windows and opened them up. This approach reinvigorated the interior, illuminating and animating the play of light on the surfaces of the building. As the designers stated:

"This was no classic refurbishment project. It followed the logic of a squat — a squatter seeking shelter in a 10,000 square meter factory building does not start wondering how to renovate the entire area. That squatter is looking for a place to bed down and feel safe."[3]

3

4

5

6

SHIHLIN PAPER MILL

PROJECT

SHIHLIN PAPER MILL:
PARADISE LOST IN TIME

DESIGNERS

INTERBREEDING FIELD

LOCATION

TAIPEI, TAIWAN

DATE

2010

"'Interbreeding' means the active confrontations of the given world structure and experimenting with different ways of transplanting, crossbreeding and hybridizing the new materials of architecture."[4]

Superuse is a strategy that utilizes found or already used objects. It is an approach to making interior space that incorporates ready-made elements into existing buildings. The fundamental intention of utilizing a superuse method is the recognition of opportunities latent in disregarded materials and the acceptance of contingency as a guide for making new elements and new spaces.

In the essay *Latent Architecture: On Interbreeding Field* Jow-Juin Ging describes how existing elements can be developed through "crossbreeding." He suggests that the processes of transplanting and fabricating found elements into existing situations is of paramount importance. In his work, these processes have a pedagogic dimension and are used as instruments in projects that enable students of design and architecture to understand building processes.

1

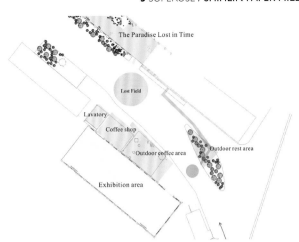

2

3

1   The journey to the pavilion is on an elevated walkway through the interior landscape of the derelict factory building.

2   The site map of the project.

3   The new coffee bar is connected to the site with a new timber canopy, sheltering drinkers on the elevated terrace.

Paradise Lost in Time is one such outcome of learning through making on-site. Interbreeding Field is a group of designers led by Li. H. Lu. It consisted of students from Tainan National University of the Arts in Taiwan. The students are engaged in live projects, jobs where they learn through doing, designing, and constructing projects on site.

Paradise Lost in Time was based in a disused factory in Taipei. The Japanese built Shihlin Paper Mill during their occupation between 1895 and 1945. After 1945 it was nationalized and taken over by the government as the Taiwan Paper Industries Co. In 1959 it became a private enterprise and was renamed Shihlin Paper Corporation. The company relocated in 1988 and the abandoned mill fell into disrepair. In the twenty-five years since it closed, the semi-ruined site was overrun by plants, creating an extraordinary interior landscape of unusual flora and fauna growing in and through the holes in the walls and roofs of the building.

In 2010, working with artist Kazuyo Sejima, Interbreeding Field transformed the factory by creating a new pavilion. "Mystery Land" was a "Paradise Lost in Time" where participants could meet and relax among the new interior landscape. A timber pavilion was constructed and strategically positioned to make use of a shaft of natural light pouring in through a hole in the roof of the derelict mechanical room of the factory building. At specific times of the day shafts of natural daylight illuminate the inside of the space. The timber pavilion was reached via an elevated walkway that meandered through the plants emerging from the floor and walls of the semi-ruined factory space.

The pavilion was designed and built by the students in order to turn the ready-made garden into a peaceful setting.

4

4 The existing trusses of the roof informs the design and structure of the bar in the old factory building.

5 New services, such as toilets, are enclosed by walls made from stacked water containers.

6 Pieces of timber are placed amongst the stacked containers in order to provide both privacy and structural stability.

In another derelict part of the factory a new coffee bar was housed adjacent to the installation. The existing structure of the building was utilized and the roof trusses were used to influence a new temporary timber soffit, protecting the customers from any inclement weather coming through the decaying roof of the existing building. This new structure incorporated an exterior timber canopy that sheltered customers wishing to sit outside. A new, elevated timber floor was designed to slide out from the interior and create a large deck for outdoor seating. It contained a ramp with which to gain access to the bar.

The reuse of the redundant spaces to house public events meant that services such as toilets needed to be constructed. Interbreeding Field and Kazuyo Sejima created a temporary enclosure by stacking plastic water containers together to make screens. Where privacy was required, the space between the containers was filled with timber, also providing structural reinforcement. At night the containers were lit to show the way to the toilets. The rigidity of the water containers also allowed them to be utilized as supports for the stools for use in the coffee bar and dotted around the site.

Interbreeding Field have subsequently worked with the site on a number of occasions. In 2011, a new generation of Interbreeding Field students and designers added "The Lost Field," a performance space in the landscape between the coffee bar and the Paradise Lost in Time. The Lost Field contained a viewing tower, a performance stage, and an auditorium that consisted of a long bench meandering through the space.

5

HAKA RECYCLE OFFICE

PROJECT
HAKA RECYCLE OFFICE
DESIGNERS
DOEPEL STRIJKERS
ARCHITECTS
LOCATION
ROTTERDAM, HOLLAND
DATE
2010

"A team of ex-convicts in a reintegration program was used for the making of the objects. In so doing, the project is more than just an example of how we can make an interior from waste, it creates added value through empowerment and education. The cost of the project is compared with an interior made of new materials and build by professional interior builders around 4.5 times lower. The project demonstrates that the realization of an interior can have more impact environmentally, socially and economically than traditional interior projects."[5]

Superuse relies on the harvesting of easily available materials. This strategy contrasts with the traditional processes of a project in which the design and realization of space is "supply" driven as opposed to "demand" driven. In other words, a superuse project is reliant on what is available at any given time.

The HAKA recycle office was designed to be built from the reuse of a variety of materials extracted from various building from around the port of Rotterdam. This process involved the research, extraction, and supply of materials to the site producing an ever-changing inventory of materials for use in the design. This contingent approach needed to be agile, as material availability changed. This was exemplified in the rethinking of the sourcing of a consignment of warehouse doors that could not be extracted due to the building being squatted days before demolition.

Built in 1932, the Cooperative Wholesale Chamber of Commerce (HAKA) building was designed by H.F. Merins in Veirhaven Street, facing Rotterdam's Lek Harbour. The building contained a factory and workshops with associated storage space for numerous goods and offices. The riverside location allowed products to be loaded onto ships and allowed materials to be loaded into the building to be held in storage silos at the top of the structure. The large Modernist building had a 23-foot (7-meter) wide bay concrete structure that facilitated large floor loadings and ensured that trains, and later trucks, could run adjacent to the building and be easily loaded from the street side. Lifts, conveyors, and chutes connected the different levels of the building, and slides facilitated the journey of the raw materials to finished goods as they descended through the building to the factory floor.

I

1 A set of elements, such as sheets of timber and doors, were designed and constructed to form an interior of contingent objects harvested from local building and demolition sites.

2 The space was organized around the frame of the building's concrete structure.

LEGEND
01—stage
02—seating auditorium
03—wall auditorium
04—showblocks
05—seating temporary exhibition
06—projection wall
07—reception desk
08—platform
09—kitchen/bar/pantry
10—meeting room

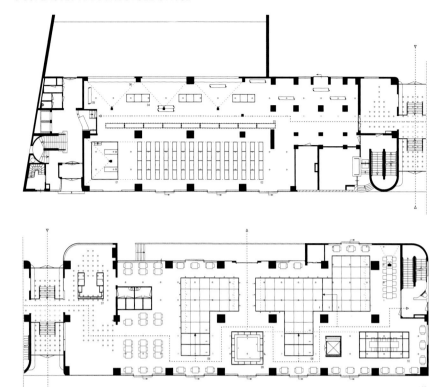

25 m   5 m   0 m

2

Since the early 1990s the building was unused. In 2009, the building was designated an "Urban Living Lab," a hub that would act as a catalyst for the area as a "clean-tech activity" space, attracting companies that would want to work by the waterside location. The first phase of the project was to design the first floor as an invitation to other possible occupants for the vacant upper floors of the building. Doepel Strijkers designed a speculative and open event space that included places to meet and work, an auditorium with an exhibition space, and places to cater for events.

The building was entered between the east and west wings via a raised platform. This new entrance was announced with a prominent glazed window, lit with striking orange, yellow, and white fluorescent lighting. The reception desk was constructed from found timber formed into a series of shelves, waiting to be inhabited with books and merchandising.

In the west wing a series of platforms marked out a temporary office space. Made from reclaimed wooden panels from a kiln in Hengerlo the platform delineated a space for an office. The kitchen was fabricated from waste materials including second-hand kitchen cabinetry and the remnants of an old greenhouse also used as canopy of the reception area. The meeting room was enclosed with 24 doors, reused from a local housing project. Set into a timber frame, the doors allow numerous entry points into the room.

3

3 Vertically hung orange, yellow, and white lighting illuminates the entrance to the space.

4 A moveable wall made from second-hand clothing separates the reconfigured auditorium (made of salvaged timber) from the exhibition space.

5 The remains of a greenhouse were combined with second-hand kitchen cabinetry to make the catering space.

6 To ensure its prominence in the cavernous space, what was left of the old greenhouse was placed atop the reception desk structure.

4

A wall constructed from 8 tons of second-hand clothing enclosed the new auditorium in the east wing. Layering the clothes into a 2-foot (600-millimeter) deep timber frame, configured as a shelving unit, provided both visual and acoustic separation. The shelving unit was designed to disappear as the clothing overlapped the edges by 2 inches (50 millimeters). The wall is on wheels and can be reconfigured when needed. The clothes have been treated so they are fire retardant and their coloring is chosen so they may be reconfigured when moved. The auditorium podium and seating was made of recycled timber slats, configured into a platform with two fold-up podiums and a series of long benches.

6

HIGH LINE

PROJECT

HIGH LINE

DESIGNERS

DILLER SCOFIDIO +
RENFRO WITH LANDSCAPE
ARCHITECT JAMES CORNER
AND PLANTING DESIGNER
PIET OUDOLF

LOCATION

NEW YORK CITY, USA

DATE

2009

"It was about thirty feet tall, and you couldn't see what was on top of it, but the rusting Art deco railings gave it a sense of lost beauty, and the spaces underneath were very dramatic; they had a dark, gritty industrial quality, and a lofty, church-like quality as well. . . . I felt what I think is the spark of most peoples interest in the high-line: wouldn't it be cool to walk around up there, twenty-two city blocks, on this old, elevated thing, on this relic of another time, in this hidden place, up in the air'?"[6]

The reuse of urban infrastructure poses particular problems. The networks and utilities that keep a city working—roads, railways, power and waste management, and so on—have to be constantly maintained and upgraded. A change in technology, whether gradual or instant, can render useless certain elements of infrastructure, and leave a legacy of often difficult or overpowering redundant relics.

Superuse is about constructing spaces with spare or excess materials. These materials can be waste or by-products taken from either demolished or no-longer needed buildings or sites. Abandoned buildings can also be considered surplus to requirements, as they fall out of use and hence they become waste. Rather than demolish, superuse can put them to good use by imbuing them with new values, ensuring that they're placed back into the cycle of value and use. This process ensures that unusual relics, industrial infrastructure, and abandoned monuments can be recycled and incorporate a new lease on life.

1

2

3

1 In its heyday, the elevated freight-train line moved goods safely away from the street level between the lower west side and midtown Manhattan.

2 Before its reuse, a landscape of exotic non-native species of flora covered the derelict elevated rail track. Photo: Joel Sternfeld

3 A series of framed views of the city punctuate the linear journey through the new park.

In 1933 the bustling trains and street traffic on the west side of New York's waterfront warehouses was alleviated by the completion of a new high-line freight track, an elevated train line designed to connect the lower west side to midtown. The High Line is a 1.5-mile (2.4-kilometer) long stretch of viaduct that runs from Gansevoort Street in the meatpacking district to West 30th Street between 10th and 11th Streets in the midtown of Manhattan. For almost thirty years trains moved goods up and down between the river and the city warehouses. The gradual change and demise of the ports, the gentrification of this side of Manhattan, and the demise in the use and efficiency of freight trains meant that in 1980 the high line was closed and left as a huge obsolete industrial monument. In 1999, Friends of the Highline was formed to resist further demolition after part of the southern end of the line had already been knocked down. They campaigned to reuse the elevated track to become an urban park, an elevated landscape that would cut through the city and become a space for the citizens of New York to idle away a few hours in a landscape raised from the hustle of the city below.

In initial visits, Joshua David and Robert Hammond, the initiators of Friends of the High Line, were fascinated by the rich and diverse flora and fauna that had grown up from the variety of seeds that had been deposited by the boxcars of the trains moving goods up and down the line. Some of the seeds were rare and had come from the ships docked in the port and were thus not native to the city. The many years of obsoletion had allowed the seeds to propagate and had turned the viaduct into a wild and unusual landscape.

The designers of the new park were impressed by this ad hoc landscape and were determined to capture the otherworldliness of this almost alien landscape that had evolved on its own 30 feet (9 meters) above the heads of passing new Yorkers. The long park is punctuated by a series of events that outline aspects of the city. The sunken "10th Avenue square" overlook frames a view up the street and gives the visitor an outline of the cars speeding up the avenue. Where the train tracks pass through buildings, coffee bars are housed under the cover of the sheltering warehouse.

4 The park can be accessed from a number of places, and is punctuated by a number of site-specific events, reinforcing its integration back into the fabric of the city.

5 The park ends abruptly at Gansevoort Street, where the southern section of the line was demolished in 1960.

6 The designers of the park seamlessly integrated the planting, pathways, and benches.

Rather than settle for the conventional path and separate vegetation model of a park a combination of new landscape elements, such as pavers and benches, were devised to integrate the landscape. Pavers were designed that could vary the relationship between path and vegetation with some integrating both or others remaining separated out. The park can go from 100 percent vegetation to 100 percent hardscape and anything in between. Park regulations enforce the prohibition of cycling, ball playing, and rollerblading, which ensures that visitors can either just walk or sit down. In a city where productivity is important, the atmosphere of relaxation is enhanced and benches and seating are positioned to allow sitting, reflecting, and watching the city below.

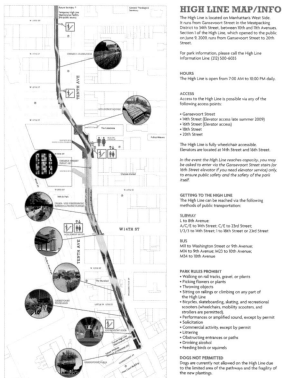

5

6

MATADERO FILM ARCHIVES

PROJECT

MATADERO FILM ARCHIVES/
CINEMA

DESIGNERS

CHURTICHAGA+QUADRA
SALCEDO ARCHITECTS

LOCATION

MADRID, SPAIN

DATE

2011

"By the end of the century concern for managing the waste created by the constant replacement of once-new products by the ever newer ones was reversing the negative charge on reuse and investing it instead with a positive moral value. Yet because the 'psychology of abundance' that accompanied the earlier 'throwaway spirit' is still prevalent, reuse is noticeably non-conformist, exceptional and ideological, rather than systematic and neutral."[7]

Recycling, reuse, and the *superuse* of materials authorizes not just the processes of salvage but also, through inference, the objects themselves. This means that the recycling of an unusual material, a building, or a space will not only endorse the selection of certain elements by their retention but it will also authenticate their value through selection and reuse. In other words as well as providing a moral value or agreeable imperative for the reduction of waste the new use is imbued with the opportunity to be exceptional, as it has been selected and recontextualised in an unforeseen manner.

In 1911, Luis Bellido designed the Madrid slaughterhouse, a huge complex of buildings in the Arganzuela district. In the 1980s the slaughterhouse was moved to the outskirts of the city and the buildings slowly fell into neglect and disuse until they were closed down in 1996. Since 2000 the *Matedero* buildings have been undergoing a radical change of use and have been converted into a campus, or a quarter for housing a diverse range of creative industries. Organized around the Calle Y Plaza Matedero, a large square linking all of the buildings in this sprawling site, are the library (La Casa Del Lector), concert space and recording studios (Nave de Musica), drop-in design offices (Central De Diseño), performance spaces (Naves Del Espanol), archives, studio spaces, and exhibition areas. Alongside these different spaces is the Cineteca, the headquarters of the Documenta Madrid Festival, incorporating a theater space and a bar (Cantina).

I

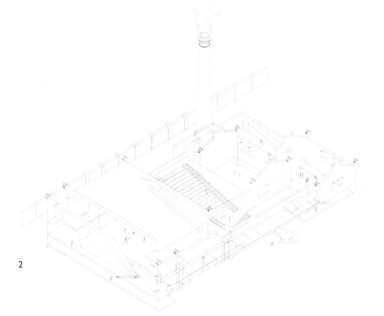

2

1 The signage on the newly cleaned and repaired buildings announces the new interior use of the old abattoir.

2 The host building conveniently accommodates the new spaces within its thick masonry walls.

3 The auditorium is enclosed within a weave of shimmering lights and hosepipes.

The buildings that were transformed consisted of a number of linked structures. They were to be adapted in order to accommodate two projection halls, film and TV studios with offices, a bar and a courtyard for open-air showings, as well as a film archive. The existing buildings were protected. So, in order to retain their appearance and character the stone façades and brick banding were cleaned and repaired. These repairs included reinforcing the foundations of the external buildings with new concrete piles and also reinforcing their structural capacities by placing steelwork into the walls to prevent cracking when new concrete floors were inserted into the buildings.

3

4

4 Gaps between the layers of the woven walls are interspersed with LED lights that animate the movement of visitors to the interior.

5 Everyday plastic hosepipes are woven around a steel framework that encloses circulation spaces, the archive, and the theater.

6 The sleek, dark, pine interior contrasts with the jagged masonry of the old building.

The designers decided to evoke the tone and characteristics of film as a device for the transformation of the atmosphere of the old abattoir. This involved the interplay of light and dark as well as the fabrication of a series of old and new montages that would sequence a spatial narrative that the visitor would experience as they moved around the building. From the outside the only indication of the change of use was the signage attached to the cleaned and repaired building. Inside, the raw stone of the building was contrasted with a dark pine timber sleeve, counterpointing the jagged masonry of the host. In order to evoke the light and atmosphere of the flickering images of film, the designers used a ready-made solution by wrapping circulation spaces and the main auditorium in a weave of garden hoses. They developed a trellis of steel rods over which they interlaced the plastic tubes. They used this same approach in order to enclose the narrow staircase and the space above the archive, as well as using it to clad the walls and ceilings of the cinema halls: giving them the appearance of huge baskets. LED lighting was worked into the construction along the load-bearing rods make the woven tubes gleam with warm orange light over three floors to the archive spaces and lend a mysterious shimmer to the dark gray woven walls of the large cinema hall before and after performances. After the film, a visit to the Bar Cantina allows guests to feel something of the original spatial atmosphere of the former slaughterhouse.

The recycling of a mundane everyday material has valorized its importance and elevated it to a substantial element in the reworking of a once odious place.

6

Notes

1. Ed van Hinte, Cesare Peeren, and Jan Jongert, *Superuse* (Netherlands: 010 Publishers, 2007) 52.

2. 'Surplus' Anna Lacaton + Jean-Philippe Vassal In Conversation with Mathieu Wellner in Petzet, Muck & Heilmeyer, Florian (2012) *Reduce, Reuse, Recycle*. Hatje Cantz Verlag. Germany. 13.

3. *Ibid* at 18.

4. From the essay "Latent Architecture: On Interbreeding Field." Jow-Jiun Ging. http://www.interbreedingfield.com/work.html accessed Aug. 27, 2014.

5. From information sent from the designers regarding the project. May 5, 2015.

6. Joshua David and Robert Hammond, *High Line: The Inside Story of New York City's Park in the Sky*. (New York: Farrar, Strauss and Giroux, 2011), 5–6.

7. Richard Brilliant and Dale Kinney, *Reuse Value Spolia and Appropriation in Art and Architecture from Constantine to Sherrie Levine* (Chichester: Ashgate, 2011), 2–3.

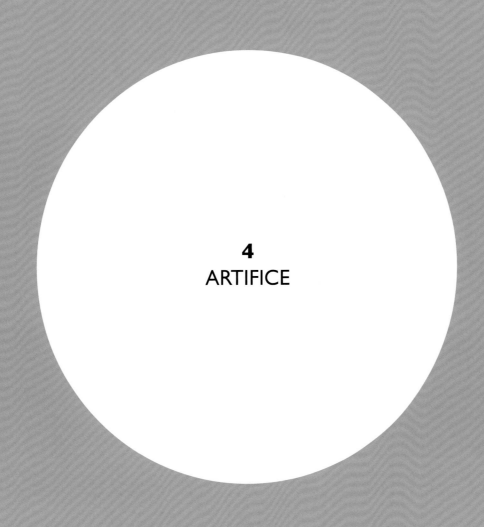

4
ARTIFICE

ARTIFICE INTRODUCTION

"In design there must always be the intention, conscious or semi-conscious, to present the actor with a legible set to act within or against. There cannot be design without intention; and it follows, since intention is a voluntary function, that there cannot be design without artifice."[1]

The *Oxford English Dictionary* describes the word *artifice* as the art of constructing, or fabricating some form of illusion. It relies heavily on the craft of the technician. It is also described as "an ingenious expedient, a manoeuvre, trick, or device." Etymologically, *artifice* is derived from the Latin word *artificium*, relating to "the employment of the art of cunning." Both descriptions suggest that by using an artifice-based approach to the design of anything ensures that the matter to be adapted will be crafted and assembled in such a way as to create an understanding with the intention to deceive, seduce, or misinform its user.

The processes of crafting and adapting existing spaces in order to accept new forms of occupation are central concerns to the designer of the interior. The employment of artifice, with which to fabricate and narrate the identity of the space, is of crucial importance. Therefore, during the conception and fabrication of an interior, when freed of the need to protect its occupants from the outside environment, the designer can conceive inside space as pure artifice. In other words, once the exterior condition is negated, or the interior is released from any environmental control responsibilities, such as keeping out the weather, the interior is liberated in order to fabricate a new, and, if required, a very contrived environment.

Therefore, an artifice-based strategy depends upon the predilections and requirements of the designer with regard to just how far they want to undertake the conceit of the environment that they are creating. Scenography and stage set design are at the extremities of artifice while at the other end of the spectrum, yet no less deceitful, are high street retail environments. Both types of spaces act as backdrops used to narrate a particular story: one helps to illustrate the story taking place on stage while the other aims to seduce you into ensuring that you part with your money. Both artifices utilize cunning and ingenious tricks to achieve their aims.

Portrait Pavilion
The fiftieth anniversary of the museum was celebrated with the design of a small, contemporary, free-standing pavilion that literally reflected the extensive portraiture collection of the ballroom in which it was placed.

UNIVERSITA METRO STATION

PROJECT

UNIVERSITA METRO STATION

DESIGNERS

KARIM RASHID

LOCATION

NAPLES, ITALY

DATE

2008

1 The free-flowing organic feel of the station is emphasized in the early concept sketch for the station.

2 The pragmatic qualities of passenger circulation, ticketing, traveling to the platforms, and egress from the station are efficiently and expediently organized.

3 Vibrant and reflective colors and materials transform the underground station into a dramatic experience for the passengers as they pass through the lobby on their way to the trains.

4 Lenticular artwork flickers and appears to move as passengers pass between the synapse-like benches.

"A subway station is a temporal, transitional space, yet the commuter is contained for a short period of time before continuing his/her journey. Our concept focuses on the commuter experience within the train station, and how the surrounding environment can serve as a respite in a day's schedule."[2]

Metro stations are usually required to be essays in spatial coherence, with the ebb and flow of passengers carefully managed and ordered. This type of space is often quantified in the safety and comfort of its passengers. Any form of artifice may be considered to be an expedient trick, unnecessary in a pragmatic and functional space where the primary concern is moving from A to B. Unexpected qualities, such as vibrant color, integrated sculpture and art work, and dramatic effect, are often not considered to be fundamental elements of a busy transport interchange.

In 2006, the expansion of a number of metro lines in Naples instigated the Stations of Art project. Also known as the Hundred Stations Plan, lines one and six of the Naples Metro would be furnished with a number of new stations filled with art installations and design work by both local and international designers and artists. The Universita station is part of the "lower stretch" of line one and runs between Via Marina and Corso Umberto 1, a central part of Naples. It was the first station to be completed in a project that has been slowed down due to the significant archaeological complexities of digging through an ancient Italian city.

In what would normally be a space solely for transit, the university context inspired the designers to create a highly choreographed, stimulating space. Rashid designed the metro station to satisfy the pragmatic requirements of the interchange but also to enable surprise and interaction with its passengers, provoking thinking and reflection as they pass through on their journeys.

1

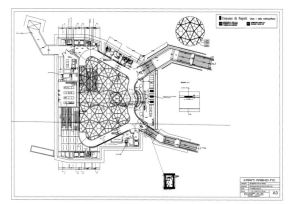

2

3

6

5 Huge sculptures, reminiscent of
Renato Bertelli's "Futurist" continuous
portrait sculpture dominate the
ticketing hall.

6 Passengers descend to the trains
via a bright blue tunnel with a top-lit,
mirrored reflective ceiling.

Apart from the metro sign at street level there is no suggestion of the qualities of
the space that the commuter is about to enter. Ensuring surprise as the passengers
descend into the station, the initial entrance spaces are covered in vibrantly colored
tiles, each one etched with a word such as *network*, *laptop*, *database*, or *software*, all
from language invented in the latter part of the twentieth century. The ticket hall
lobby level further emphasizes the difference between the piazza above and the
new underground atmosphere below. The designers lined its back wall with a backlit
lenticular icon artwork that changes color and perspective as the passenger moves
through the space. The surreal atmosphere of the hall is heightened by a series of
sculptures, placed among the routes through the space. Overscaled floor-to-ceiling
reproductions of Renato Bertelli's "Head of Mussolini" sculptures provocatively
dominate the space. In-between them is a series of silver benches, representing
overscaled nodes in the synapses of the brain. Lime green walls, deep blue floor
tiles, and a white ceiling with a recessed zigzag lighting system complete the optically
and mentally stimulating appearance of the environment.

The descent to the trains from the lobby is via an escalator in a blue tunnel with a
mirrored ceiling. From this space the passenger arrives into the bright pink platform
lobby. Platform steps feature abstracted portraits of Dante and Beatrice. The bright
and vibrant colors are used as tools for finding one's direction. The accent colors of
lime and pink indicate the direction of travel and guide visitors through the station
and to the trains.

The platform level of the station is where Rashid lets the dynamic of the train
animate the space. Passengers can take a seat on small, organic-shaped benches.
The walls of the platform feature backlit artwork. As well as providing lighting for
the space they show animated films to the commuters passing by on the trains.

STUDENT ACTIVITY CENTRE

PROJECT
STUDENT ACTIVITY CENTRE
(SAC)
DESIGNERS
SUPERMACHINE STUDIO
LOCATION
BANGKOK, THAILAND
DATE
2013

"I like elements which are hybrid rather than 'pure,' compromising rather than clean, distorted rather than 'straightforward,' ambiguous rather than 'articulated,' perverse as well as impersonal, boring as well as 'interesting,' conventional rather than designed, accommodating rather than excluding, redundant rather than simple, vestigial as well as innovating, inconsistent and equivocal rather than direct and clear. I am for messy vitality over obvious unity. I include the non sequitur and proclaim the duality."[3]

The deployment of artifice as a strategy for reusing existing buildings is a process that requires the designer to employ cunning as well as expediency in order to realize the project. The altering of anything in order to house something it was never intended to house requires the instigator to approach the project with some degree of innovation. An artifice strategy may be deployed when the host space is tasked with a new use that requires such a drastic transformation of its qualities that the form of the new occupation will dramatically alter the existing building, making it virtually unrecognizable from its previous function. Utilizing an artifice-based approach ensures that the new occupation of the building will misinform the user of the original function for which the existing building was originally prepared; creating a new hybrid space where its past is present but only as a shadow of its former self.

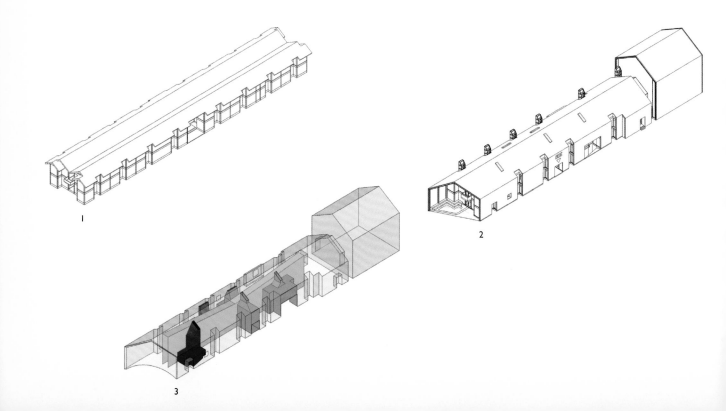

1

2

3

4

1 The housing block before its transformation.

2 After its adaptation: The new roof created a taller and more inviting space. A new entrance is carved out of the end of the building and the gym is attached to the rear.

3 The central, public corridor is the main circulation artery of the interior, linking all of the rooms and activities.

4 The new, cedar shingle-clad exterior is adorned with super-sized graphics. The graphics are designed to invite students into the space to participate in the activities within the building.

The adaptation of the Student Activity Centre (SAC) at Bangkok University by Supermachine Studio required the adaptation of a twenty-year-old, long, thin student dormitory wing. The housing—290 feet (90 meters) long by 82 feet (25 meters) wide—contained thirty-two rooms and twelve internal courtyards. The two-story building was long, low, and dark, and in need of repair after the Thailand floods of 2011. Its mundane qualities provided the inspiration for Supermachine to transform it into a vibrant space where it would become a center for the students of the university to indulge in a diverse range of out of classroom activities. These activities ranged from cheerleader training to music studio rehearsals and even a Thai dance club.

The initial part of the project required the overhaul of the external fabric of the building. The double-pitched roof of the existing building was removed and a new single-pitch roof was created. The new roof was covered with cedar shingles and finished with large, painted diagrams of the activities happening within the space, creating a single material skin and sending an inviting signal to the students on the campus. Merging the two roofs into one heightened the central circulation space, creating a much more generous public corridor, the main artery of the complex. In order to maximize internal light this circulation route was painted in a vibrant yellow. Eight of the twelve courtyards were filled to make room for the new programs, while the remaining four were geometrically modified, made public, and painted in vibrant colors including purple, green, pink, and turquoise. Natural light was brought in through the courtyard skylights to ensure that the new space was bright enough and pleasant enough for students to spend time in. Tacked onto the rear end of the building was a completely new structure. The 52-foot (16-meter) high gym is used for larger group activities as well as being the training ground for the internationally famous cheerleader team of Bangkok University.

The housing block, once the place of quiet study and repose, has been radically altered to become the main attraction of the campus and the site of all types of diverse and energetic activities.

6

7

5 Breakout spaces, inviting students to take a rest, are painted in a vibrant fuchsia. Suspended net "baskets" punctuate the axial route through the building.

6 The vibrant yellow corridor animates the interior space.

7 Each activity is located off the central circulation route.

FOUQUET'S BARRIÈRE HOTEL

PROJECT
FOUQUET'S BARRIÈRE HOTEL
DESIGNERS
MAISON EDOUARD FRANÇOIS
LOCATION
PARIS, FRANCE
DATE
2006

"The cult of originality inhibits treating copying as a serious activity. In other art forms, parody might seem less of a dubious undertaking. Picasso said 'Copy everyone except yourself.'"[4]

The art of deceit and the strategy of artifice are useful instruments for the retention and reuse of *valuable* existing buildings. While often considered to be a conservative approach to designing buildings, "fitting in" to a city in a sensitive, urban context requires careful thought and consideration. The trick of mimicking the surroundings in order to disappear or blend into a context can be considered to be a radical strategy for adaptation, especially when the copy supersedes the uniqueness of the original from which it has been derived.

In an architecturally sensitive location on the Champs Élysées in the center of Paris, the Groupe Lucien Barriere bought the celebrated Le Fouquet's restaurant. Subsequently, the business acquired the rest of the block around the restaurant in order to construct a luxury hotel around the renowned eating establishment. The entire site consisted of seven buildings. The façades overlooking the Champs Élysées were authentic Haussmann and were protected. Two buildings on the Avenue George V and Rue Vernet were built in the 1980s, yet they were designed and built to imitate two nineteenth-century neo-Haussmann and neo-Louis Philippe styles. A 1970s bank building with a smoked brown glass façade completed the block.

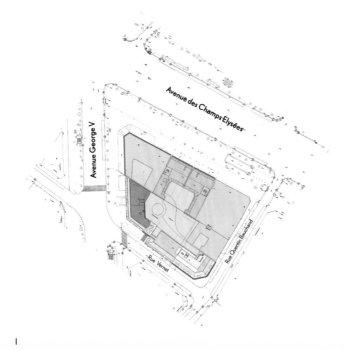

1

1 The block in plan showing the copied and pasted facades highlighted in red.

2 The new floor levels of the hotel rooms demonstrate the impact upon the façade through the imposition of what appears to be a randomly positioned set of windows.

In order to transform the disparate collection of buildings into a luxurious hotel the seven buildings were adapted and then linked with a new subterranean service structure. This service structure consisted of a system of corridors and spaces that created direct links to each of the 107 rooms, reinforcing their expedient and efficient servicing at top speed by 350 staff. Other high-class amenities required for a destination hotel included a new spa, built into the old shopping arcade in the block, and the redevelopment of the Le Fouquet's restaurant. Along with other bars and social spaces, a series of gardens built into the gaps between the seven buildings in the internal courtyards of the block completed the luxurious destination. These green spaces gave the hotel guest access to manicured and elegant miniature gardens set in the center of the city.

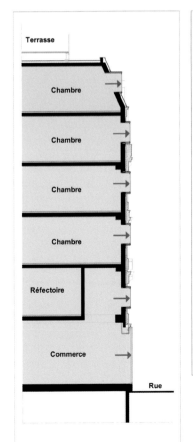

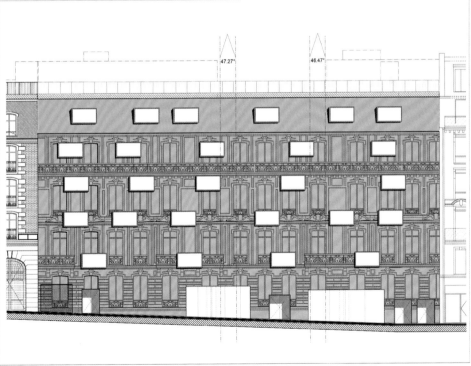

2

3

3 Elements such as new doors adopted the style of the façade yet were made in a new material such as steel.

4 The new façade is constructed from gray concrete blocks, castings of the copied Haussmann original.

5 The abrupt endings of the new façade covering emphasizes its wallpaper-thin appearance. Like a "curtain wall," the façade is like a decorated drape hung across the front of the buildings.

6 The windows of the hotel rooms irreverently puncture the façade and heighten the contrast between the old building and its new use.

The client required that the designer unify the seven façades on the block, creating a statement building in the city center. The Paris heritage commission was watching closely to see what was proposed to the protected Haussmann-style façades, and in particular where the original restaurant was located. In this sensitive context and position, the designers decided to adopt a strategy of artifice: a strategy that perplexed the heritage agency yet was approved for its sheer audacity. Francois decided to mimic and copy the protected façade and apply it to the other parts of the block. This approach ensured it would unify them with the Haussmann façades, as the new would be a copy of the old. This was taking the logic of "in-keeping" to a new degree of proficiency.

Utilizing this discrete approach to the valuable Haussmann façades, they copied them and applied them as a unifying cover, or mask, to the rest of the block. The Le Fouquet's façade was digitally scanned and then cast in a series of gray, concrete-block reliefs. The glass façade of the 1970s building was removed and the concrete-block relief panels were applied to this frame and the other buildings. Where the internal levels of the hotel no longer corresponded to the new façade details, new windows were punched out of the concrete skin. The disjunction between the copied ornate façade, with its friezes, architraves, stringcourses, and window details, and the new windows, is profound. The sharp contrast of the frameless, glazed window panels, letting natural light into the rooms, signals a surreal junction between the old and the new.

4

5

6

PORTRAIT PAVILION

PROJECT

PORTRAIT PAVILION

DESIGNERS

PAULIEN BREMMER

ARCHITECTS + OFFICE

JARRIK OUBURG (CO+OB)

LOCATION

VOORSCHOTEN,

NETHERLANDS

DATE

2010

"In Freudian theory the mirror represents the psyche. The reflection in the mirror is also a self-portrait projected onto the outside world. The placement of Freud's mirror on the boundary between interior and exterior undermines the status of the boundary as a fixed limit."[5]

In the essay "The Split Wall: Domestic Voyeurism," Colomina describes how, in a similar fashion to Freud's study, Adolf Loos's houses deliberately obscured relationships between inside and outside. Loos would often use a mirror placed in a particular position to disrupt the threshold between the interior and the exterior in order to heighten the interplay between the actual and the virtual, reality and illusion. The use of artifice as a strategy for building reuse often relies on tricks, or elements that can deceive or make ambiguous normal spatial relationships. The inversion of the relationship between inside and outside is one of these illusions.

Duivenvoorde Castle dates back to the early thirteenth century and is one of the oldest castles in the Netherlands. Its current appearance is as a result of modifications made in the nineteenth century. Since 1960, it has been a museum, containing seventeenth- and eighteenth-century portraiture silver and porcelain collected by the Duivenvoorde family. To celebrate the museum's fiftieth anniversary, a pavilion was commissioned with which to observe the rituals and history of portraiture, updating perceptions around the significance and role of image and connecting a new generation of museum visitors and social media users to the ideas of personal portraiture.

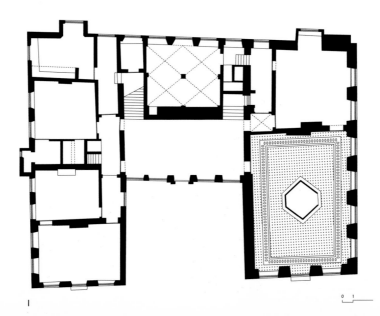

1

1 The hexagonal free-standing pavilion is placed in the center of the ballroom.

2 The mirrored surface of the element refracts light across the room, adding to the illusion of its dimensions and further confounding its presence in the space.

3 Extruded from the pattern of the carpet, at night the small space entices visitors into its softly lit interior.

The new pavilion was located in the ballroom of the castle. Dating back to 1717, the elaborately decorated room is attributed to court architect Daniel Marot and is designed in a unique Louis XIV style. The ornately paneled room contains a number of life-sized portraits of the successive generations who lived at the castle. In its entirety the museum has a collection of 131 family portraits on display, spread over the different halls and rooms of the castle.

2

3

4 The hexagonal-shaped pavilion almost seems to disappear among the grand opulence of the baroque seventeenth-century ballroom.

5 The interior of the room is lined with 131 portrait facsimiles with space included for contemporary additions to illustrate the cultures and role of portraiture in modern times.

Inside this unique environment the designers created a reflective pavilion, an object that not only disrupts the relationship between inside and outside but one that allows visitors to see themselves in the context of the room and the paintings around them. The form of the pavilion is drawn directly from the surfaces of the room; its hexagonal shape is an extrusion of the central pattern in the existing ballroom carpet upon which it is placed. The exterior of the pavilion is clad with acrylic sheets with a mirroring surface. Because of the reflection, the interior of the baroque room becomes an even more excessive space whereby the pavilion, ballroom, visitor, and portraits visually merge into one complex image, disrupting the relationship between object and subject, portrait and person.

Inside the pavilion, the walls are covered in reproductions of the 131 portraits in the castle. All portraits are scanned, reproduced in black and white, and suspended on the brightly lit walls of the pavilion, forming the basis of the exhibition. In an attempt to reconcile notions of historical image-making through portraiture and the virtual collection of lives on social media sites such as Facebook, visitors are invited to bring a personal portrait and add a contemporary layer to the pavilion, connecting seventeenth-century image making and their contemporary equivalents.

4

UNA HOTEL VITTORIA

PROJECT
UNA HOTEL VITTORIA
DESIGNERS
FABIO NOVEMBRE
LOCATION
FLORENCE, ITALY
DATE
2003

"We do not have to dig so deep. After all, to explore the white wall is precisely to explore the surface itself. But the surface is far from superficial. Details matter. Textures are telling."[6]

The strategy of artifice relies heavily upon the development of particular surface identities. The projection of a series of particular material and atmospheric appearances—conditions such as color, light, touch, and look—is the instrument through which identity is portrayed. In the reuse of existing buildings, this type of identity construction is often reliant on the choice of a particular palette of materials and surfaces, elements that project meaning and convey a particular atmosphere. The construction and imposition of a series of materials upon a space is a process that forms a backdrop for its users to occupy and undertake their daily lives. It is a procedure that forms one of the fundamental concerns of the design of the interior.

The UNA Hotel Vittoria in Florence is located in a listed building on the banks of the river Arno. The exterior of the building could not be changed; therefore, from the outside its appearance is left untouched. The restraint shown on the outside of the building contrasts with the exuberance within. Novembre designed the hotel interior to be unique, and he created an inimitable interior that he felt could be the beginning and the end of a visitor's experiences of the city. Therefore, the dramatic quality of the interior is emblematic of the city; elements taken from history, details of the urban fabric, materials extracted from the surroundings are absorbed and reworked to create a series of elements and spaces that introduces the visitor to Florence.

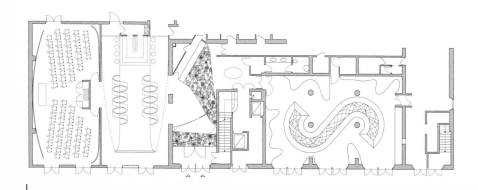

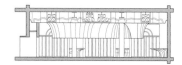

1

1 Each room of the first floor of the hotel is dominated by its furniture arrangements and is conceived as a different "sample" of the urban context.

2 The protected and sober exterior of the hotel is in stark contrast with the exuberant interior within.

2

The first introduction to the city begins in the reception of the hotel. Visitors pass through the front doors and are immediately enclosed by a huge spiraling, sculptural ribbon that rises from the floor of the lobby then loops across the ceiling and back down to form the reception desk. The strip is covered in floral-patterned tiles. The mosaics reference the regal villas and the flora of the countryside that surrounds the city. The recurring theme of the loop is a motif that is repeated in the adjacent bar area. This time the form is upholstered and races across the room in the form of two parallel spirals. The loop is a motif used to symbolize the theatrical aspect of the city but, more pragmatically, brings guests together in one piece of furniture. Novembre designed the hotel to act as a stage on which visitors could relax as well as socialize and meet each other. The furniture is emblematic of this.

The sociable aspect of the project continues in the restaurant. A large curving table that slides through the space dominates the dining room. The city is quoted throughout the hotel by the designer utilizing elements inspired by a local Tuscan monastery. A stained-glass ceiling light reflects the sinuous curve of the table. Novembre obtained the licenses to eighty-four portraits of Florentine people from the Uffizi Gallery. In order to develop the corridors of the hotel—spaces that Novembre considered the weak parts of hotel design—each of the eighty-four rooms is entered through an upholstered Florentine portrait door. As guests pass through the corridors to their rooms they reenact what many of the visitors would be doing on their journey through the city's art galleries and cultural spaces.

The surfaces of the hotel are emblematic of the city in which the visitor is a guest. Novembre uses artifice as a method of allowing each visitor a sample of what they are about to see when they journey into the city.

3 Upon entering the hotel the visitor is enclosed by a mosaic-tile-encrusted ribbon that guides them straight to the reception desk.

4 Inspired by Tuscan monastery furniture, the restaurant is arranged around a long, curved table that is top-lit with a stained-glass lighting element.

5 Two floor-to-ceiling, upholstered spiral loop seating elements encourage interaction among the hotel guests.

4

Notes

1. Joseph Rykwert, *The Necessity of Artifice* (London: Academy Editions, 1982), 59.

2. Cited in Information pack sent by the designer, May 31, 2014

3. "Non-Straightforward Architecture: A Gentle Manifesto" Venturi, Robert *Complexity & Contradiction in Architecture.* (London: Butterworth Architecture, 1966), 16.

4. Fred Scott, *On Altering Architecture* (Abingdon, Oxon, Routledge, 2008), 75.

5. "The Split Wall: Domestic Voyeurism," cited in Beatriz Colomina, *Sexuality & Space* (Princeton Architectural Press, 1992), 86.

6. Mark Wigley, *White Walls, Designer Dresses. The Fashioning of Modern Architecture* (Boston, MIT Press, 2001), 15.

5

5
INSTALLATION

INSTALLATION INTRODUCTION

"Sometimes the host building is little more than a stage for the performance of the objects but the best installations actually expose and reveal the beauty and qualities of it, allowing it to be read and understood in its own condition. The installation will enliven and reveal the true, possibly hidden or lost character of the building."[1]

An *installation* can be a single object or a series of objects; it might be a concept, a performance, or a temporal or permanent space. It could be site-specific or noncontextual. Whichever way, and by however means, it is formulated, the strategy of installation is founded upon all of these ideas. Installation can be utilized in order to construct an "event" based strategy, one where the development of the extraction of drama and a heightened contrast between the existing and the new is of paramount importance. Installation incorporates the development of both non-site-specific and site-specific elements, elements or spaces that can often be deemed temporal and often that are not built-to-last: a condition that sometimes means that they are constructed with their own demise incorporated into their very being.

A contemporary installation phenomenon is the "guerilla" or "pop-up" space. Now virtually a spatial cliché, this spatial typology encapsulated the installation ethos by improvizing maximum impact with minimal means. Other installation types include large- or small-scale event design, such as trade shows, along with scenography, exhibitions, and retail spaces all designed to structurally impact upon the existing building as little as possible, yet to impose maximum impact upon its users. Once the installation or interior has exhausted its impact potential or is deemed to have become unfashionable, or simply if the duration of the event is over, then it is usually uninstalled as quickly as it was constructed.

Significantly, installation does not always place emphasis on the crafting of the object. Instead the speed in which the idea needs to be realized is of paramount importance. Therefore improvized materials, ready-made found objects, and other such contingent materials are often used to quickly realize an idea. The careful consideration of such elements, if chosen well, can also heighten the impact of the installation.

The fundamental aspect of this approach is that an installation-based strategy will usually do two things: It will set out to heighten the drama between itself and the environment in which it is placed, and it will emphasize its content rather than the way in which it was constructed. If it is site-specific, the designer will achieve the enhancement of the environment in which it has been placed through the distillation of its qualities.

Duomo Cathedral Museum
The new museum is carefully ordered around a route through the twenty-six rooms that circulates a visitor through the museum, which displays the sculptures and works from the cathedral, and back to the same starting point without them ever repeating the same route.

NOMA FOOD LAB

PROJECT

NOMA FOOD LAB

DESIGNERS

3XN ARCHITECTS

LOCATION

COPENHAGEN, DENMARK

DATE

2012

"An Installation differs from a conventional architectural design in several ways: It is temporary, that is, its demise is planned from the outset; its function turns away from the utility in favour of criticism and reflection; and it foregrounds the content."[2]

The design of environments in which to prepare and consume food can sometimes reflect the ephemeral pleasure that is inherent in the enjoyment of a well-made meal. While considered to be the lesser element of the act of eating, drinking, and socializing, the careful and considered creation of a particular aesthetic and atmosphere are vitally important components, central to the enclosure of the act of making and eating food. Installation is a strategy that can be used to create these types of event-based environments, places where space can be utilized as an instrument for the enhancement and aestheticization of the food experience.

Since 2010, the Michelin two-star restaurant NOMA has been voted one of the best restaurants in the world four times. A play on the Danish words *Nordisk* and *Mad*, NOMA is renowned for its innovative gastronomy. Above its ground-floor restaurant, and situated in an eighteenth-century, protected, historic warehouse in the Christianshavn neighborhood of Copenhagen, the designers were commissioned to design NOMA's test kitchen: a food lab that will facilitate the experiments of its fifty chefs, food innovators who ensure that NOMA keeps producing ground-breaking Nordic cuisine.

1 The simple, exposed surfaces of both the existing building and the elements of the new interior reinforce the philosophy and aesthetic of NOMA's approach to cooking.

1

2 The complex construction drawings and processes of the circular storage units around the columns belies their apparent simplicity.

3 The central circulation ensures that there is clarity and distinction between movement and working areas in the large room.

2

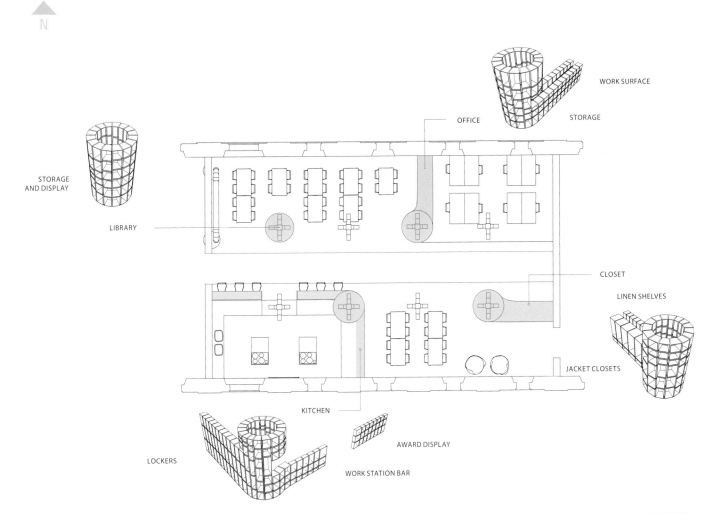

3

4 All of the workspaces, including the test kitchen, are positioned at the edges of the room in order to maximize natural light.

5 The herb garden was placed adjacent to the test kitchen and is on hand for the chefs. Like the new storage elements, its simplicity in construction belies the fact that all of the furniture was designed using parametric modeling software.

6 The food lab is on the second floor of the warehouse, above the renowned restaurant.

Renowned for using ingredients only sourced from Nordic countries, the regional approach to NOMA's cuisine was re-emphasized by the designer's sourcing of local plywood for the project. The protected warehouse context meant that nothing could be permanently fixed to the surfaces of the building. In particular, the internal structure, consisting of eight timber columns, had to remain free of any permanent additions. With both of these constraints in mind, 3XN created a series of free-standing installations, objects at a scale between the monumental proportions of the warehouse and the furniture requirements of the chefs.

Four cylindrical units were designed to alternately wrap the columns, of which three had extensions of double-sided storage units. With a delicate touch these were connected to the walls of the space. These units split the 2,200-square foot (200-square meter) room into four areas: dining, kitchen, office, and storage. These were designed to be discrete, but also planned to overlap with each other. The furniture was cut from regular sheets of Nordic birch and Spruce plywood, and then assembled on site. The project was completed from start to finish in just three weeks. The open-fronted shelves and storage were designed to hold the plastic containers that the chefs used for their spice library. This storage system externalized the results of their research in the "experimentarium." It was anticipated that the boxes would hold the exotic and unusual spices that the chefs develop and will then be placed alongside artifacts and objects that the chefs will use to inspire them in their trials. When full, the shelving will become an open library of spices, books, ideas, objects, and images inspiring the ingenious testing going on around them.

A central route through the lab facilitated straightforward circulation and ensured that the workspaces were placed near the windows, bathing them in natural light. An indoor herb garden ensures adjacency to the test kitchen. The staff canteen seats fifty and is regarded as an opportunity for all of the workers, regardless of position, to sit and try the food of the restaurant together. A daily event that included the sampling of the gastronomic experiments.

4

5

6

HEAVYBIT INDUSTRIES

PROJECT
HEAVYBIT INDUSTRIES
DESIGNERS
IWAMOTOSCOTT
ARCHITECTURE
LOCATION
SAN FRANCISCO, USA
DATE
2013

"Technological advances mean that for the first time in a century the knowledge worker's equipment is no longer heavy and tied to a desk (adding machines, telephones and computers), but lightweight, portable and mobile, providing constant connectivity that is independent of place."[3]

Creating an interior for something as ephemeral and transient as cloud computing technology requires the initiation of a spatial aesthetic that will offset the momentary and short-lived. Yet it needs to convey solidity and strength. This balance of representing the discernible and the invisible creates a distinct set of problems for designers: What is the aesthetic of something that is all about speed, time, and disappearance? What does a workplace need to be when technology has rendered obsolete many of the requirements of the traditional office building?

Heavybit Industries is a cloud computing software developer. It is a company that incubates digital start-ups for nine months in order to foster business development in this fast growing industry. When Heavybit decided to create a new headquarters in San Francisco's "tech corridor" they deliberately chose a serious, solid, masonry-bonded warehouse: a building that would compensate for the fleeting nature of the business taking place inside of it. Heavybit wanted to convey the solid, engineering aspect of software development. While the development of cloud technologies suggested ephemerality, the developers proposed that this type of engineering is infrastructural. Like the laying of new roads and utilities, it is not glamorous but it is highly essential.

Lisa Iwamoto and Craig Scott (IwamotoScott) were commissioned to turn the warehouse into an incubation space, one that would host embryonic software development companies for a period of nine months. The interior of the building needed to facilitate the new companies and also promote networking, helping each company to develop through sharing ideas, best practices, and the constant refinement of their products. The three-story building was already restored and cleaned. The owners had sandblasted both the inside and outside of the shell of the building. This blank canvas prompted the designers to utilize an installation-based approach to the reuse of the existing building—a strategy that resulted in the construction and installation of a series of lightweight, budget-conscious elements, such as office spaces and furniture, that would foster interaction and facilitate the work of the embryonic digital start-ups in the space.

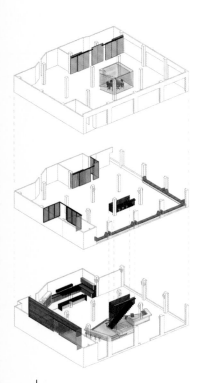

1

2

1 A series of elements were installed throughout the three-story building. The elements were designed to facilitate the various functions of the workers and the nascent companies.

2 The simple, solid, masonry and glass exterior of the warehouse counterpoints the light, ephemeral nature of the digital technology work that is being undertaken inside.

The designers placed the main workspace on the third floor. The first floor became the main social space. The second floor was designed to provide an even balance between socializing and working and act as the link between the first floor and third floor. The designers increased the connection between the first and second floor with a new staircase. Centrally placed in the large main workspace, and situated in-between the concrete frame structure, the lightweight steel mesh stair was designed to appear as though floating among the heavy masonry and concrete structure of the building. From the front, the steel-plate risers look substantial, yet from the side they almost disappear. The intended weightlessness of the stair was designed to look both floating and heavy at the same time—an appropriate metaphor for the project.

The first floor is the most open and social space of the building. In the center of the space IwamotoScott designed an angular plywood platform that accommodated a variety of functions. As well as a stair platform, and continuous benched seating area, it was designed to become a podium for guest speakers and a reception desk for visitors as they enter the building. The far end of the platform folds up to become an "idea bar" for hosting informal meetings and discussions. The whole object appears to be hewn from the ground, as the plywood was laid on edge to give the appearance of a series of stacked sheets. The heavy appearance of the platform lends the room a spatial "anchor," as it sits firmly in the center of the space. Breakout spaces, such as a conference room and a collective dining room with serving area and kitchen, complete the open, social role of the first floor.

3

3 A woven, mesh light fixture based on the hexagonal Heavybit logo, was designed for the first floor conference room.

4 The open-plan first floor, arranged around a stacked-effect plywood platform, facilitates seating, presentation space, stair landing, and ideas bar within its folded and angular geometries.

5 Polycarbonate screened meeting spaces surround the rope-enclosed third-floor meeting space.

Open-plan workstations and breakout spaces dominate the second floor. A long, thin upholstered bench that runs the full length of the space is positioned under the windows. It invites workers to sit in the natural light. Where possible, the robust masonry, concrete, and timber interior was offset with lightweight materials. Polycarbonate screens enclose second-floor conference rooms. They let the light in but retain some privacy from the open-plan space. In the center of the third floor the designers focused Heavybit's limited budget on making a meeting space enclosed with walls fashioned from rope and electrical conduit, which are stretched across a steel frame and suspended from the ceiling.

The designers constructed a carefully composed interior that balances the intangible elements of the cloud with the solid realities of twenty-first-century workspace requirements.

4

5

RED BULL MUSIC ACADEMY

PROJECT
RED BULL MUSIC ACADEMY
DESIGNERS
LANGARITA NAVARRO
LOCATION
MADRID, SPAIN
DATE
2012

"The act of introducing something new to a space—something physical like an object or an installation, or temporal like a drama or a performance—can have the most profound effect. . . . With the introduction of the installation or the performance, the space, (the interior) becomes a frame for something else, and that frame establishes a set of conditions by which the new element can be experienced, judged, and given meaning."[4]

As well as drawing attention to itself, a reuse project that uses an installation strategy will often highlight the context in which it is placed. It is the manipulation of this *resonance* between elements and space that enables the designer to generate the character and quality of the installed project as well as emphasize the attributes of the host building.

The Red Bull Music Academy (RBMA) is a nomadic annual music festival. For the last fourteen years, this event has been held in a different city. It connects eminent participants in the music industry to a network that allows them to experiment and exchange knowledge about the latest advances, technologies, business, and ideas in the industry. The 2011 edition of RBMA was going to be held in Tokyo, but due to the devastating effects of the Tohoku earthquake, the location had to be quickly changed. With only five months to plan, the city of Madrid offered a vacant warehouse space in the Matadero Madrid complex. Once the abattoir of the city, the Matedero is now a cultural center with exhibition spaces, a theater, a cinema, and a library. Unit 15, a large empty shed in the complex, was used to house the academy. The only stipulation was that new academy had to leave the 51,000-square foot (4,750-square meter) warehouse exactly as it found it, and that all aspects of the academy buildings could be recycled.

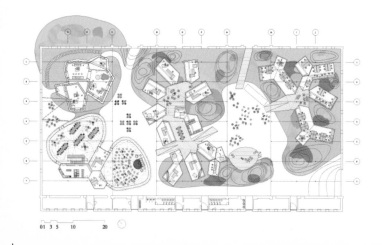

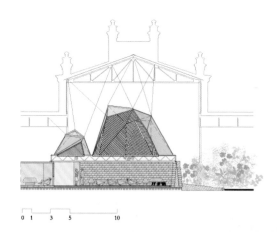

1

2

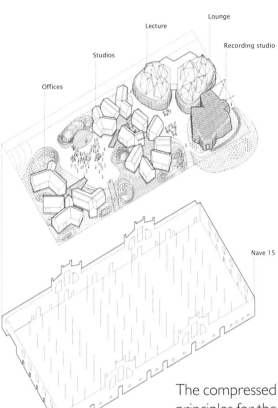

Offices

Studios

Lecture

Lounge

Recording studio

Nave 15

3

1 The mixture of landscape and pavilions, arranged organically inside the space, gave the impression of a bucolic and pastoral setting within the former abattoir.

2 The only physical connections to the building were the temporary supports for the suspension of the fabric roofs of the lounge and lecture spaces.

3 The village of pavilions were organized organically around the orthodox and ordered structure of the warehouse.

The compressed time scale of the project required a set of very particular clear principles for the design. All construction needed to be lightweight and able to be completed in just two months. Every aspect of the project had to be reversible, in other words it could be broken down and taken away very quickly or redeployed easily amongst the rest of the Matadero complex. Finally the building was to be left exactly as it was found.

Unit 15 provided a large, open space comprised of a steel structure with a brick façade. This structure opened directly to the outside. To realize the academy, four areas were required: offices; studios for musicians; recording studios; and an area used for conferences, radio station, and as a lounge.

In the short space of time, the designers created and fabricated a small city of independent pavilions within the cavernous steel frame of the warehouse building. The installation resembled a village, in which the community of users could meet and interact. As well as the networking and performance requirements of the space, the acoustic qualities of the pavilions, and the spaces between them, were of paramount importance. The pavilions were constructed from timber allowing the inclusion of thick acoustic interiors with which to control sound. Their placement around the perimeters of a number of meeting and performance areas ensured that they acted as acoustic baffles for the stages. The social and performance area acoustics were enhanced by their enclosure with a series of soft and absorbent surfaces. Black sandbags were stacked around the areas to baffle sound, and cloth domes were hung from the ceiling.

The temporary nature of this project required that it be designed to be dismantled in such a way so as to not leave a trace. Even the "heaviest" elements were designed to be reversible, and to allow for their easy recycling for future events. Even the potted plants used in the gardens were later transplanted in other areas of the Matadero or the city.

4 The new pavilions of the academy were organized around the columns of Unit 15, counterpointing the regimented steel structure of the existing building.

5 The autonomous timber structures did not touch the existing building, ensuring minimal sound transference between them and also allowing the host structure to be returned back to its original state when the academy was finished.

4

5

6 The sandbag-lined lounge was enclosed with a dynamically striped canopy, ensuring high quality acoustics inside the space.

7 The interior of each pavilion studio was equipped to facilitate the generation of ideas and sounds for the musicians.

6

7

DUOMO CATHEDRAL MUSEUM

PROJECT
DUOMO CATHEDRAL MUSEUM
DESIGNERS
GUIDO CANALI
LOCATION
MILAN, ITALY
DATE
2014

"When an exhibition, a stand or a showroom is prepared, or when work or living spaces are fitted out, when a play or an opera or a ballet is staged, what is constructed is a piece of the city. A piece of the city that can be regarded as belonging to its most highly evolved fringe, one responding to the logic of reversibility, adaptation and the refunctionalisation of the constructed world."[5]

The design of a museum in a particular historic context often entails a forensic examination of the existing building. Such an examination can ascertain changes to the building and help determine how the alterations might be utilized. This process can often involve the uncovering of new artifacts and finds, often secreted in the fabric of the building and covered up by centuries of later use. It is within this context that the strategy of installation can be used to create a dynamic and informative museum interior, one that relies on the innovative juxtaposition between the existing environment and the artifacts being placed within it.

The Cathedral Museum exists in the huge edifice of the Palazzo Reale (royal palace), adjacent to the Duomo in the center of Milan. The Palazzo Reale was first called the Palazzo del Broletto Vecchio, and was the seat of the city's government

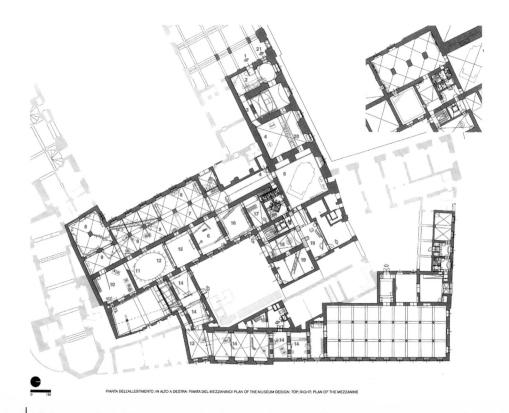

PIANTA DELL'ALLESTIMENTO; IN ALTO A DESTRA: PIANTA DEL MEZZANINO/ PLAN OF THE MUSEUM DESIGN; TOP, RIGHT: PLAN OF THE MEZZANINE

1

1 The plan shows the complex sequence organized within the twenty-six rooms of the museum from the start to the finish of the journey.
    1—Entrance
    5—Model of the cathedral
    7–9—Origins of the cathedral
    10–15—16th century
    16–18—17th century
    18—18th century
    19—19th century
    20—20th century
    21—Exit

2 In order to facilitate the successful design of the museum, 1:10 and 1:20 scale models of the rooms and the objects were simulated in Canali's studio.

2

during the Middle Ages. Part of the palace was demolished to make way for the construction of the fourteenth-century cathedral, forming the *Piazzetta Reale* or the Small Royal Square, adjacent to the Duomo.

The museum houses artifacts from the cathedral and has been in existence since the 1950s when its first iteration occupied ten rooms of the palace. The museum was doubled in size in 1974 and remained open in this configuration until 2005. Guido Canali was commissioned to redesign the new museum. He enlarged the space, allowing many more works to be displayed in an intricate and carefully considered route through twenty-six rooms of the palace. During construction, Canali uncovered various layers of the building that were covered up in the 1773 renovation by Giuseppe Piermarini. These included the infilling of a series of medieval arches from the first version of the early palace.

As well as uncovering some of the changes in the building, Canali utilized some of the original ideas from the 1950s museum that were lost in the 1970s alterations. He reinstated the 1950s entrance that was adjacent to the busy Piazzetta Reale. This ensured that visitors to the popular large-scale palace exhibitions would see the Cathedral Museum.

Once inside the entrance a carefully worked out route through the twenty-six rooms circulated a visitor through the museum and back to the same starting point. This was done without the visitor ever repeating the same path. The interior was organized in a chronological fashion, starting with artifacts from the Visconti and Sforza eras, through to the sixteenth century, then the Borromeo era. The seventeenth-, eighteenth-, and nineteenth-century rooms finished with the twentieth-century room before the exit.

3

3 The journey begins and ends with the monumental sixteenth-century, wooden, scale model of the adjacent Duomo.

4 Many of the larger rooms were split to become part of the route moving through the museum and the journey coming back. Objects, as well as a low guiding rail, were installed in a way to facilitate this journey.

5 Archaeological excavation of the building exposed the various layers of its construction. The designer opened old in-filled arches in order to frame the views through the interior space.

6 In order to heighten the power of the objects they were often installed clustered together in groups.

Canali enhanced the journey by utilizing a rhythmic installation approach. This sequential device ensured that passage through the rooms was compressed and expanded space was prioritized. This was manifested in corridor aspects of the route with recessed or linear display cabinets counterpointed with large, open rooms filled with sculptures, often clustered together on stands or screens for maximum effect. The next spatial sequence would then carry on with linear corridors to be followed by another room and so on. Like a journey through the streets of Milan, the museum interior is constructed to be similar to a piece of the city in which it is located.

The installation begins and ends with the impressive sixteenth-century scale wooden model of the Duomo, an astoundingly detailed replica of Milan's most famous building, which is located just across the street. It is a replica of the constructed piece of the city that visitors will interact with on their visit to the city, a building that, like this museum, has changed considerably over time and will carry on adapting to changes in the future.

4

5

6

GROENINGEMUSEUM

PROJECT

GROENINGEMUSEUM

DESIGNERS

5IN4E

LOCATION

BRUGES, BELGIUM

DATE

2003

1—Conceptual art
2—Primitive art
3—Renaissance
4—Baroque
5—Neo-Classical
6—Belgian
7—Archive
8—Late Nineteenth Century
9—Expressionist
10—Abstract
11—Late Twentieth Century
12–13—Lobby Entrance

"Installation can be seen as the generation of a symbiotic relationship between a building and the series of elements placed within it. The two often have quite different characters and it is their juxtaposition that provides life and vitality for both."[6]

The design of spaces in which to exhibit artifacts tasks the designer with the appropriation of the existing building and the consideration of its use as either a neutral or a subjective backdrop. Museum spaces are also often designed with the dual requirements of being both private, allowing the quiet contemplation of the object, and also public, affording a civic space in which to gather citizens and represent the institution. The understanding and then the implementation of all of these conditions can create intriguing interior spaces. The strategy of installation can afford the designer the vitality of their juxtaposition and the richness of a spatial diversity through the temporal placement of objects, rooms, elements, and people.

Entered through a discrete alleyway, and hidden away in the center of Bruges, the Groeninge Museum was built in the 1930s to house a collection of six centuries of Flemish masterpieces. The existing building was designed by the municipal architect Josef Vierin, and was constructed within a surrounding walled garden. It was designed as a series of rooms encountered *enfilade*, as the visitor moved through them. The secluded nature of the museum meant that by the late twentieth century it had become overlooked. It was in need of an update in order to ensure that it remained relevant and that a new audience could access its important collection.

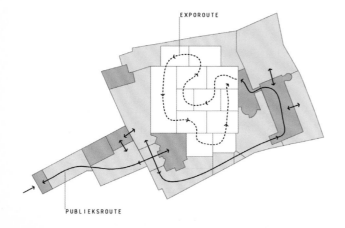

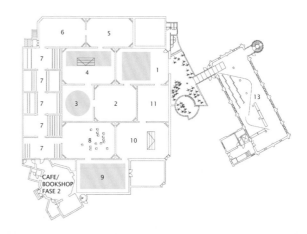

1 The public routes and the exhibition routes work together to connect the museum back to the city and transform it into an inspirational destination for viewing Flemish masterpieces.

2 The new route through the rooms is interrupted by the archive, to the left of the plan, which is placed in the middle of the journey, and is designed to allow the visitor to reflect on the history of Flemish art.

3 The designers used mesh racks on the archive walls to allow unusual and unplanned connections to be made between the paintings hanging on the screens and the viewers among them.

In 2002, 5 IN4E was commissioned to redesign the museum. They proposed that the underwhelming condition and experience of the space could be reversed through implementing two things: a rethinking of the museum's relationship to the city and a reworking of the interior rooms and the displays within them.

In response, 5 IN4E proposed two new routes through the museum. One route was known as the "public" route. The other was called the "exhibition." The public route connected the visitor with both the city and the museum by opening up the garden. It brought visitors into and through the garden, and deeper into the complex of museum buildings. This journey through the landscape not only enhanced the enjoyment of the walk but also heightened the sense of anticipation of seeing the new museum interiors as the path through the gardens led the visitor deep into the site and to the entrance to the museum.

The second part of the strategy was to reorder the interior with careful consideration given to the visitor's journey and experience in each of the rooms. First, the enfilade of rooms was carefully reoriented and a new chronological order to the paintings was implemented throughout the interior. The journey started with Primitive works, then Renaissance, Baroque, and neo-Classical. The visitor then encountered the nineteenth and twentieth century with sculptures and landscape works drawn from expressionist and abstract styles, finally arriving at artwork from the beginnings of the twenty-first century.

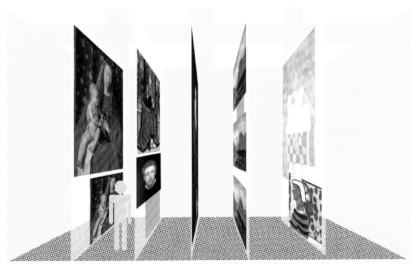

3

5 Numerous black and white DSR chairs populate the landscape room, affording visitors a number of different viewpoints from which to view the art.

6 An overscaled, mosaic-tiled terrace gives visitors the chance to look at paintings from high up or low down in the room.

4

4 The open archive allows visitors to access six centuries of Flemish paintings in a different context and setting to the rest of the museum.

The designers applied a strategy of maximum impact to the installation of each room. This relied on the density of paintings and artifacts that were on display. This approach ensured that each room created a significant effect upon the viewer, one that changed as they drifted between each room and each style of work. This dramatic impression was heightened by a series of elements that were installed in each space in order to enhance this symbiotic relationship. A room with hard, white, mosaic-tiled floors in one space would be contrasted with a room with bright red carpet in the next. In the Abstract Expressionist room, an overscaled, tiled "terrace" allowed visitors to sit or to stand in order to get a better view of the art. While the next room was overpopulated with numerous black and white Charles and Ray Eames DSR chairs, in which to sit and ponder the numerous landscape paintings arranged in close proximity on the wall. Whether hard floor or soft carpet, sitting down or standing up, each room was designed to allow the visitor a contrasting view of the art.

In the middle of the chronological route was the archive. This was a breakout room designed to educate the visitor through six centuries of Flemish art. The paintings were unceremoniously hung on a steel mesh frame, allowing the visitors to make connections between different works while introducing them to the art at a totally different pace to the rest of the museum.

Notes

1. Graeme Brooker and Sally Stone, *Rereadings-Interior Architecture and The Principles of Remodelling Existing Buildings* (London: Riba-Enterprises, 2004), 127.

2. Sarah Bonnemaison and Ronit Eisenbach, *Installations by Architects – Experiments in Building and Design* (New York, Princeton Architectural Press, 2009), 14.

3. Jeremy Myerson and Philip Ross, *Space to Work* (London: Laurence King, 2006), 13.

4. "Installation and Performance," David Littlefield. Cited in Graeme Brooker and Lois Weinthal, *The Handbook of Interior Architecture & Design* (London: Bloomsbury, 2013), 226.

5. Branzi, Andrea. "Exhibition Design as Metaphor of a New Modernity" (Lotus International, 2002), 162. Cited in Graeme Brooker and Sally Stone, *From Organisation to Decoration: An Interiors Reader* (Routledge, 2013).

6. Graeme Brooker and Sally Stone, *Rereadings-Interior Architecture and The Principles of Remodelling Existing Buildings* (London: Riba-Enterprises, 2004), 127.

5

6
NARRATIVE

NARRATIVE INTRODUCTION

"The recent approaches to narrative design have emphasized the importance of the visitor experience. So called 'experience design' emerged in the commercial sector. It is focused on the individual visitor and perceived as a question of 'messaging.' . . . Inevitably, a range of cross-over technologies tend to be employed to generate these often theatrical environments: immersive interactivities create a kind of narrative experience that can adjusted, as it were, by the visitor."[1]

Emerging from the Latin term *gnarus* knowing, and thus *to know* is by extension to narrate, *narrative* is described in the *Oxford English Dictionary* as the process of recounting or reciting a tale, or a story. The expression, or narration, of an account of space informs the fundamental characteristic of the adaptive strategy of narrative. An environment that is designed to recount and enhance a specific or number of stories about objects, spaces and their inhabitants can be derived from utilizing a strategy that augments the existing space's story-telling potential. In contrast to a new-build environment, existing spaces will often have a previous history, a series of facts, or a fictitious past that can be extracted and transcribed into three dimensions. This is just one narrative component that can be utilized in the design of a new interior using this approach. As well as the history of a place, its new use can also be a generative instrument in the formation of narrative material. For instance if the project to be placed in the adapted building is an exhibition, the way in which the material is thematically structured and then sequenced in space, can form the basis of the narrative of the exhibition. This curated story is usually a thematic and highly ordered ensemble of artifacts for the visitor to interpret and ultimately consume. As David Dernie suggests, a range of technologies, ideas, and designs can be used to create immersive, interactive narrative environments where the visitor can adjust or edit his or her own version of the story that is being communicated.

A narrative approach to the adaption of existing buildings can include the inscribing of consultation into the processes of making new interiors. It can also be used to incorporate source material from the existing building, a process akin to a type of spatial quoting from the very fabric of the space.

Strategy is a device that will drive a conceptual idea and will be able to act as an organizational tool. When utilizing a narrative strategy, concepts and organization can be enhanced through understanding the motives of the user of the space and the particular information that is needed to be relayed to them by the interior and its contents. Whichever way narrative is used as an approach to adapting the existing environment, it enhances the continuous stories of a building's past, present, and future. In simple terms, the strategy of enhancing and developing the narrative of an existing environment can lead to unique interior spaces that are impossible to replicate in a new-build project.

Shoah Memorial
The "wall of indifference" greets visitors to the Shoah memorial. It poignantly reminds them of the complicity of the citizens and of the building in Milan's history. The journey into the memorial is facilitated by a steel walkway, itself a potent metaphor of transition and movement for the narrative of the interior space.

SHOAH MEMORIAL

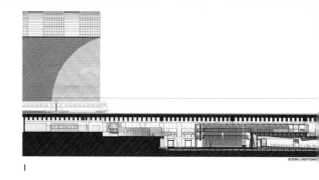

PROJECT

SHOAH MEMORIAL

DESIGNERS

MORPURGO DE CURTIS

LOCATION

MILAN, ITALY

DATE

2009–2016

"I believe that in a place like this, new interventions cannot blend in, and that they can make a decisive contribution to the space but they should never, in any way, be mixed up with its qualities. In general, I like this severity, the fact that in the memorial there is never a sense of abandonment nor a comment on the tragedy of the deportation."[2]

The commemoration of stories through the utilization of space, as an instrument of remembrance, is a process that is conditional, and one that is based upon the account that is to be told and the raw material of the site. In such a context, the designer becomes the editor of the material: each idea, and subsequently each design idea, is reliant upon the development of an appropriate narrative and context. It is always a complex process, raising questions of whose narrative is being relayed and how is the story being told? It is also an approach that imparts huge symbolic meaning upon all of the aspects of the project. Every feature, from conceptualization to the particular choice of materials, is scrutinized for meaning, some of which may or may not have been intended. Therefore the designer becomes both the strategist and the manipulator of each element and material of the project, many of which will impart much more significance than its immediate appearance may imply.

The winning competition entry for the new Milan Central Station by the architect Ulisse Stacchini was started on site in 1912. The building opened in 1931 and was subsequently adopted as a symbol of fascist power by the newly installed Italian Prime Minister Benito Mussolini. The station contained twenty-four tracks covered with a monumental 656-feet wide by 236-feet high (200-meter by 72-meter) glass and steel vault, a record at the time. The station façade was constructed in a melodramatic mixture of Liberty and Art Deco, and was embellished with grandiose statues, creating a suitably bombastic edifice for the Italian dictator.

1   Long and short section through the basement memorial with the monumental arches of the train station roof overhead.

2   Plan and section of the place of reflection.

3   Plan of the memorial space, the place of reflection is located in the top right hand corner.

1

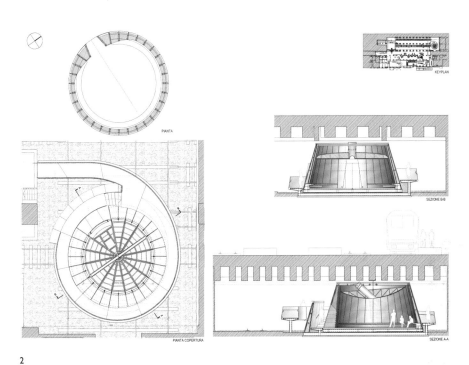

2

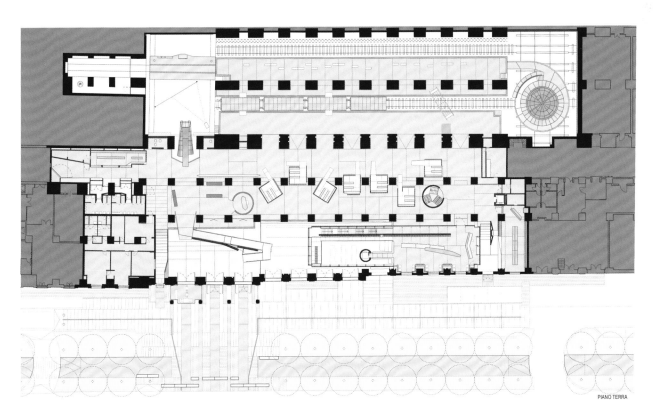

3

4

Away from the front of the station and its busy entrance, in the lower levels of the platforms and in the deepest recesses of the east side of the station, a train track was constructed for the adjacent post office building. It was a line that could efficiently and quietly transport sacks of mail from the building onto the expansive rail network. Between 1943 and 1945 this track was utilized to forcefully deport Milan's Jewish residents, sending them to various concentration camps including the notorious Auschwitz. The deportation process involved people being brought to Milan's San Vittore prison and then transported to Milano Central. Then, they were loaded into a boxcar and lifted up onto the main track where the carriage was hooked up to a train and taken from the city. The cargo of people was loaded in the early hours of the morning in order to ensure that there were no witnesses, and to avoid hindering the daily operations of the mail and other cargo. The documentation of this tragic episode in European history, and the role of this space in its execution, constitutes the material presence of the new Shoah Memorial. Due to its sensitive nature the project has taken almost ten years to come to fruition and only now is near to completion.

The project was realized utilizing a series of found and constructed elements. These components order the narrative of the memorial and through their qualities make legible the harrowing story of its history. The elements were organized around the platform where the victims were transported. Four empty boxcars were left in situ as reminders of the story. They are objects that resonate with meaning and history and are deliberately placed to ensure that the visitor constantly views and returns to them as they traverse through the space.

4 An artist's image of the walls of books and readers in the library. Its placement will provide an animated window to the outside world and will symbolize awareness and the ongoing study of Jewish culture.

5 The names of the 2,000 deportees are illuminated on a video projection wall viewed through the empty boxcar.

5

The cavernous undercroft of the station was stripped back to expose the raw concrete structure of the building. The severity of this visceral interior shell was then distinguished with a number of robustly designed new elements. Upon entering the space visitors are met with "the wall of indifference," a slate-gray colored concrete wall that explicitly spells out the Italian response to its history in this process. Placed at the edge of a significant change in floor levels, (the height of a loading bay) the visitor ascends a ramp toward a void before a thin glass balustrade safely guides them from the edge of the precipice, back behind the gray wall and up into the main area of the memorial. This symbolic journey dramatically alters its direction, signifying the unexpected passage that many of the detainees would experience as they were led to the boxcars.

On this journey into the memorial visitors view the library, located in the three-story void, facing the window of the memorial. When finished, the walls of books will be visible to passersby outside the memorial. The library is meant to symbolize ongoing Jewish culture and the future of the memorial. Once finished, its steel frame will resound with banks of books and learners, reading and writing and exploring texts and animating the words of the past.

The main section of the memorial contains the halls of records, a series of enclosures relaying testimonies and holding archives. These are positioned against the backdrop of the timeline and the wall of names, individually documenting the 2,000 names of the deported. At the far end of the track is the place of reflection, a corten steel cone deliberately positioned at the eastern end of the space. The enclosure represents a stopping point and a moment of reflection on the memorial. It is an isolated and quiet space, set apart from the constant rumblings of the trains in the still working station: a constant reminder of the journeys being undertaken above the memorial space.

The four remaining empty boxcars show how the wagons were loaded and then shunted into the elevator and lifted up onto the tracks to be transported to the camps. Their position is a constant reminder of the harrowing narrative of the Shoah and its memorialization in Milan.

6 The corten steel enclosure affords the visitor some peace and reflection amid the constant rumble of trains on the tracks above the memorial.

7 The upper and lower levels of the space are linked with a new staircase enclosed within a cylindrical concrete cylinder.

LULLABY FACTORY

PROJECT

LULLABY FACTORY

DESIGNERS

STUDIO WEAVE

LOCATION

LONDON, UK

DATE

2013

"Narrative is itself a kind of cognitive mapping, and the crises of representation associated with the modern, and especially the postmodern condition, present challenges to the effectiveness and aims of narrative."[3]

Narrative or storytelling is a strategy that can be used to enhance neglected or overlooked spaces. It is one method of extracting character from a nondescript or undervalued environment, such as a service yard or alleyway between buildings. Then it can be used to celebrate the fact that while considered dull or lifeless, each space has some kind of character (however deeply that might be submerged). Sometimes the most extreme imagination has to be used in order to develop the spatial mapping of a new place, especially for an audience that needs to be enchanted by storytelling and fantasy.

In London, Studio Weave have reworked a slither of a small space between buildings in order to help young patients in Great Ormond Street Children's hospital to marvel at their surroundings and distract them from the arduous processes of their recoveries. Over the next 15 years the hospital will be undergoing a significant urban transformation. A new park will replace the Southwood building and new medical facilities will be constructed around the edges of the new green space. This slow transformation means that the Southwood building will need to remain in operation while the new buildings are constructed around it, effectively enclosing it and hemming it in until it becomes obsolete and can be demolished. So far, the initial stages of this process have produced a series of awkward spaces around the building. What was once concealed, such as service walls and ducts, has now been exposed. Ironically, as the new modern buildings are erected around the Southwood, the floor to ceiling glass walls of the new medical buildings frame the previously hidden aspects of the back of the building, aggrandizing their mundanity as they appear as newly framed unintentional works of art.

Previously hidden and now on show to the recuperating patients in the ward Studio Weave was commissioned to enliven the grimy back façades of the Southwood building. Rather than sweep away the tangle of ducts, pipes, and services encrusting the walls after years of changes and use, the designers took great pleasure in these ad hoc sculptures. Instead of demolishing or covering them up, they constructed a story around the idea that in order to lull the children in the hospital to sleep at night large amounts of soothing lullabies would be needed. What if this once unprepossessing service alley was the place in which these lullabies could be manufactured?

1 The lullabies can also be heard on the in-hospital radio network.

2 Floor-to-ceiling glass walls of the new children's wards frame the views of the lullaby factory.

1

2

3

4

5

3 The ductwork, trumpets, and tubing of the new sculpture combine with the old service ducts and piping to create a vertical garden of sound and delight.

4 The sculpture cannot touch the ground nor touch the new façades of the adjacent wards.

5 Ground-level horns produce an audible lullaby composed by sound artist Jessica Curry.

Hence the Lullaby Factory was conceived. The site for the factory was itself a challenge. At 98 feet (30 meters) long, yet in places just 3 feet (1 meter) wide, the alleyway was both unusually shaped and intimidating. In addition, no new element could touch the floor or utilize the new façades of the adjoining contemporary ward buildings. Therefore the buildable area was limited to just the back of the Southwood building. Studio Weave initiated the project by surveying the site. They mapped the space using a 3-D scanner, building up an accurate digital model of the existing space—ducts and pipes included. Then they fabricated their lullaby factory with a network of pipes, trumpets, dials, and horns. This framework of ducts, valves, and gaskets created enough sound for a magical chamber orchestra of sounds and stories to be generated for passersby as well as a visual spectacular for the children in the adjacent wards.

Constructed by artists and piped into the system of trumpets and ear horns, the lullaby factory comes with its own enchanting history, a narrative developed by the fictitious character of Mr. Lambert Echo and his Whispersonnel. Patients can also tune into the hospital radio to listen to them. Rather than deploy the tired and overused language of gaudy colors and rudimentary forms, so often associated with children's objects and spaces, the designers instead opted for something much more sophisticated. The ducts and pipes and trumpets are exquisitely detailed, with brass and gold pipes joined to spun-aluminum trumpets and metallic finished bronze-like tubing. Their appearance is akin to the vertical workshop of a mad professor or inventor.

The best views are given to the patients themselves. The factory is framed on all floors by the great expanses of glass covering the new buildings. One day this will all be gone as the building is demolished, but for now children can watch the stories and sounds being fabricated and transmitted via pipes and plant works in the overlooked back alleyway that has become a childlike vertical magical garden.

FAI-FAH

PROJECT

FAI-FAH

DESIGNERS

SPARK ARCHITECTS

LOCATION

BANGKOK, THAILAND

DATE

2012

"The centre was built on a budget and is skewed toward selling ideas to kids—ideas about imaginative engagement, creative output, self worth, and future possibilities." [4]

During the design process, various forms of consultation will take place. This is usually when clients, building users, communities, and other stakeholders outline a range of ideas and concerns. In these meetings common goals are often explored and developed. Quite often some of the outcomes will find their way into the new designs. It is through engagement of this kind that the clients, building users, communities, and stakeholders invest in the design and become intrinsically connected to the project, particularly when they have played an active role in its design. It is these shared narratives and common goals that reinforce the connections between a building, its interiors, and its users. These collective narratives are valuable links between the users, their requirements, their identities, their ideas, and even sometimes their dreams.

The Thai Military Bank (TMB) commissioned Spark to design its new Fai-Fah building in Prachautis, a suburb in the south of the city of Bangkok. The Fai-Fah program teaches arts and life skills to disadvantaged children, offering them free classes in music, painting, drawing, design, gardening, martial arts, dance, and cooking. Volunteer bank staff usually undertake the teaching, and each center (this is the second) is funded by the generosity of the bank.

This project was housed in two adjacent traditional shop house units, both of which where owned by the TMB and subsequently leased to the center. Like a terrace or townhouse, and usually three-stories high, a shop house is a traditional Asian housing type with a shop on the lower floor and accommodation above. The building is located on a busy main street in the suburb of the city, and rather than appear discrete the building was designed to stand out. It did this with an imposing crisscross, steel, latticed façade, with its name attached to the front in large illuminated letters. At street level, a series of rotating boxes displays the work of the children. The façade served no purpose except to unify both buildings as one, and to announce the center to the city. Even the original balconies, now covered with the new screen, were finished in a series of bright garish colors so they would stand out to the passersby below.

1 The unification of the two shop houses is completed with the new façade and the services block attached to the back. Each floor is opened up with the removal of the party, or adjoining, wall between the buildings and the addition of a new structure.

2 Long section through building shop house and party wall.

1—ART INSTALLATION
2—ENTRY
3—LIVING ROOM
4—WORK STATION
5—UTILITY
6—COURTYARD
7—GALLERY
8—LIBRARY
9—STORE
10—STAFF ROOM
11—BALCONY
12—SCREEN & SIGNAGE
13—VOID
14—LOUNGE
15—WET AREA
16—ART STUDIO
17—DANCE STUDIO
18—POTTERY CLASS
19—ROOF GARDENS
20—TANK ROOM

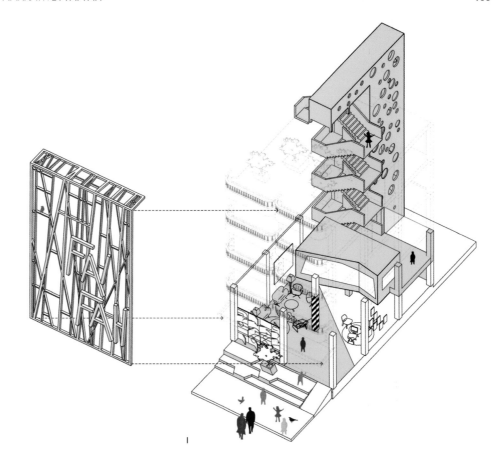

1

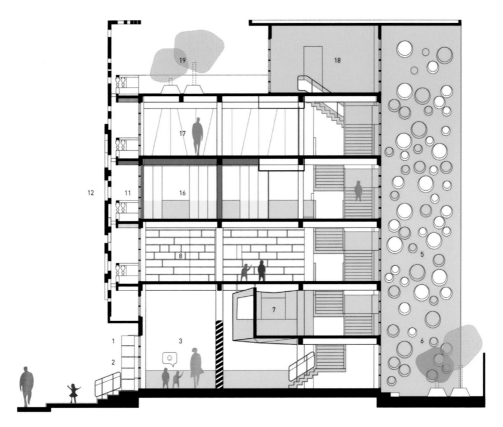

2

4

3 The first floor "living room" and mezzanine gallery is finished with vibrant yellow resin floor and walls and a black and white hazard stripe column.

4 The vibrant façade is reminiscent of an abstracted set of ladders, reflecting the progression made by the children in the program.

Rather than establishing a discreet presence the center is proud of the role it plays in the lives of the children that use it. Spark embraced this inclusive approach and they engaged the children of the center very early on in the discussions of the project. They set up a series of workshops asking them what they liked and disliked about the program and most importantly asking them to draw their ideas. Subsequently, the façade was developed in consultation with 30 children from the first Fai-Fah center in Pradipat. The form and vibrant appearance of the second center subsequently emerged from the energetic discussions about how the building should look and how the interior should represent the exterior. The designers drew their influences for the façade screen from a series of children's drawings that showed ladders as a metaphor for progression. The center was perceived as a place of mobility: one where the children felt it would help them to move onward and upward with their lives. Therefore, the ladder became the motif and symbol for the exterior representation of the center to the city, a sign of upward mobility for the kids.

The word "fai" translates as electric or spark and "fah" means blue (the corporate color of the TMB). The color and energy of the name and of the children's drawings prompted the designers to use bright and vibrant colors throughout the interior. The first floor "living room" with a gallery mezzanine was finished with a bright-yellow resin floor. The new structure, replacing the demolished adjoining or party wall between the two shops, was finished in a vibrant black and white hazard stripe. The second-floor library and meeting room and the third-floor art studio were also brightly colored. The fourth floor contained a dance studio complete with its own sprung floor. On the roof, a garden was protected from the sunlight and breeze by the shading overhang of the "ladder" façade. The restricted size of each floor impeded the addition of any services, so a yellow bubble-patterned service core containing a stack of toilets and a tank room was attached to the back of the building. Some of the bubbles were punched out to make windows for the bathrooms.

The ladders, bubbles, and vibrant colors ensure that the children have a place that resembles their desires and needs. They have played a significant role in the creation of the center, a place that will give them a chance for a considerable start in life and which, through the development of their stories and narratives, has empowered them to invest emotionally in their space.

DANISH NATIONAL MARITIME MUSEUM

PROJECT
**DANISH NATIONAL
MARITIME MUSEUM**
DESIGNERS
BJARKE INGELS GROUP (BIG)
LOCATION
HELSINGOR, DENMARK
DATE
2014

"Narratives that personify ethical or existential questions have profoundly shaped our understanding of space. . . . Within the framework of these spatial geometries, narratives can engage with the medium of space, and form the basis on which architecture can be given meaning."[5]

As an approach to a design, and in the hands of the right designer, a narrative strategy can be used to accentuate the symbolic rendition of objects, elements, and space in order to emphasize a particular story or history. Narrative is a device that can be used for the designing of interior spaces where particular collective memories or histories are required to be externalized and depicted. Using a narrative strategy often results in the abstraction of a key element or theme of the project, place, and site, often rendering it in a contemporary manner and in such a way as to stress a distinct idea or meaning of the project and its location.

The Danish Maritime Museum is located on the edge of the Oresund Strait, adjacent to the Kronborg Castle, a UNESCO World Heritage Site and the place of the previous museum. In the early 1980s Helsingor Vaerft, the shipyard that employed 4,000 local people (10 percent of the population of the town), was closed. This catastrophic event prompted a rethink of the site and also of the town's attitudes toward its built environment heritage. A master plan of the infrastructure of the docks instigated a series of landmark projects designed to reimagine the area as a tourist destination. One project was the "Culture Yard" by AART architects, a 183,000-square foot (17,000-square meter) cultural and knowledge center that included concert halls, showrooms, conference rooms, a dockyard museum, and a public library, all housed in the retained and remodeled shipyard buildings.

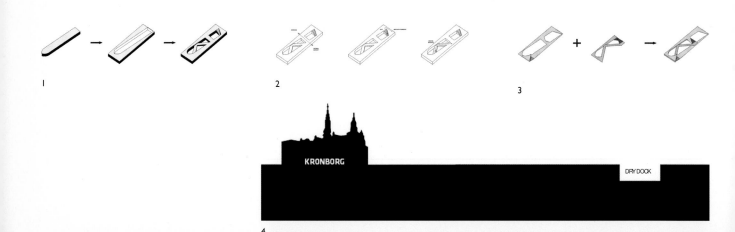

1   2   3

KRONBORG   DRY DOCK

4

1/4 The conceptual and strategical basis of the project.

5 The Kronborg Castle that faces the Oresund Strait dominates the UNESCO World Heritage Site. The museum is to the east of the adjacent culture yard.

6/7 The symbolic shape of a boat was reinstated in concrete into the excavated dock. The museum was then placed in the space between the walls.

5

6

7

8

9

10

8 Bridges and ramps, the design language of ships and the sea, are used to circulate visitors around the museum.

9 The display cases are designed to appear as though they are floating around the backdrop of the wide expanses of the sea.

10 The exhibition displays all aspects of the contemporary maritime trade, such as food containerization and distribution, among the sloping floors of the museum spaces.

The Maritime Museum was another significant element of the master plan. It was a project that involved the reoccupation of one of the disused dry docks. The heritage conditions of the site, with its close proximity to the castle, meant that the new museum needed to be as unobtrusive as possible. Therefore B.I.G. made the decision to submerge the museum down into the depths of the dry dock. All that could be seen from the first floor was a glass balustrade, keeping unsuspecting visitors from dropping 8 meters into the depths of the empty quay. The museum began with the excavation of the dry dock, widening it to its outer limits and then rebuilding the evocative ship-shaped walls of the wharf in thick concrete. Large expanses of glass were then used to create windows that punctuated the thick walls and which let light into the museum rooms behind. The exhibition spaces were then placed in the gaps between the void and the wider dock walls. The huge 492 × 82 foot (150 × 25 meter) void at the center of the museum was designed to represent an enigmatic and symbolic shaped boat, a constant reminder of the illustrious and busy past of the shipyard.

Another key symbolic element of the project was water and the life upon it. The emblematic form of the museum was augmented by the manner in which the visitor experienced the museum. A series of undulating ramps and bridges, the language of ships and of a sea-faring culture, were deployed to circulate visitors around the museum. The inclined plane of the bridges and ramps, stairs, and corridors pitches the visitor through and around a series of exhibition areas that contains cases and displays that also undulate and roll through the space. The museum was accessed via a descending bridge that zigzagged across the dock and into a lower-level foyer. The visitor was then circulated around the periphery of the museum, through each of the rooms, ascending to the lower level of the space, while always being able to make reference through the glass windows, to the central void of the dry dock and the symbolic representation of the history of the shipyards, their workers, and the town.

C-MINE CULTURAL CENTRE

PROJECT

C-MINE CULTURAL CENTRE

DESIGNERS

51N4E

LOCATION

GENK, BELGIUM

DATE

2010

"The design refrains from making an iconic addition to the old complex, as envisaged by the original master plan. Instead it sets out to make manifest the qualities of the existing complex by continuing and completing the organisation, borrowing its details, appropriating its principles."[6]

Remodeling industrial buildings incorporates a number of central themes regarding the adaptation of existing buildings to incorporate new interiors. Industrial buildings, such as factories, mines, steelworks, and power stations, usually embody a large amount of information regarding their previous uses, the lives of the people who have worked in them, and how they have been changed and adapted over time to incorporate new technologies. The often robust nature of the buildings means that they have usually been changed radically over time, with the building being treated as a mere receptacle for the work that has gone on inside and around it. They can be treated with irreverence and due to their robust nature are often able to accept radical changes. Industrial buildings are often also important indicators of the social and communal lives of their occupants and families and cities in which they are placed. They will often be the container for numerous workers and very often placed at the center of their respective communities. They will be markers of economic fortunes and can often be indicators of success and failure in trade, markets, government policy and regulation. They will often be large scale and occupy huge tracts of land, some of which they might contaminate. Their regeneration or demolition completes the cycle of perceived value. All of this information provides the narrative material for the designer to emphasize or suppress when they are reworking the building.

The C-Mine project reworks the energy buildings of the complex that forms the Winterslag mine of the Limburg coalfield in Genk. Closed in 1988, the building was empty for many years until it was reactivated as part of a master plan for the site. In contrast to many new-build environments, existing spaces will often have a history, a past that can include different uses and a patina that these different occupations will imprint upon the interior. These layers of time, and their traces, can be extracted and subsequently used to influence the new use. Rather than fetishize the layers of occupation, 51N4E decided to build upon the existing, and complete out what they saw as a building that could accept radical change. The building was to be redeveloped as a cultural center, with exhibition, design center, and auditoria. The main additions were two large aluminum-clad theater blocks. Rather than adhere to the master plan of the site, the designers located the blocks in the angles of the T-shaped building, making them look like natural additions of the building and therefore accretions of the next stage of its development.

1 This concept sketch shows how the designers contradicted the master plan and instead of an iconic and separate edifice they built the auditoriums alongside the main hall of the energy buildings.

2 The robust structural logic of the building's lower floor reinforced the new layout that ensured that the auditoriums were placed on either side of the central hall.

3 The T-shaped aspect of the building can be seen clearly in the upper level plan of the center.

4 Two new auditoriums, rising from the plinth of the existing building, were placed within the terraces of the building.

1

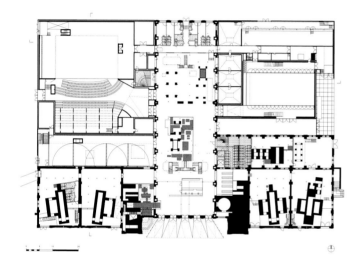

2

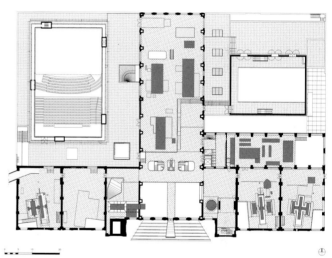

3

4

5 The new, black, steel "funnel"
entrance to the center.

6 The continuation of the red
and white tiled flooring unified the
disparate elements of the upper level
of the main hall of the energy building.

6

The main hall, complete with turbines for powering the workings of the old mine,
was retained and utilized as the entrance and circulation as well as exhibition space.
Indicative of the resistance to creating an iconic or overpowering addition to the
building, was the continuation of the red and white tiled floor of the complex.
The designers sourced and replicated the existing tiling and continued it onto the
terracing that surrounds the external forms of the auditoriums outside of the
building. The unbroken surface united the disparate series of both interior
and exterior elements. The addition of a new black steel "funnel" entrance
counterpointed the rooftop water tower and clearly distinguished the way into
the building.

The extracted narrative material of the building has enhanced the strategy of
developing this environment and has led to a series of unique interior spaces,
unrepeatable anywhere else.

Notes

1. David Dernie, *Exhibition Design* (London: Laurence King, 2006), 23.

2. Umberto Riva, "Neither An Abandonment Nor A Comment".
    Abitare Magazine. No 530. January 2014, p. 69.

3. Robert T. Tally, *Spatiality* (Oxford: Routledge, 2013), 74.

4. Yabuka, Narelle. 'Bright Spark'. Architects Journal 06/09/12, p. 36.

5. Nigel Coates, *Narrative Architecture* (Chichester: Wiley-Academy,
    2012), 14.

6. Peter Swinnen, *51N4E Double or Nothing* (London: AA Publications,
    2011), No page number.

7
ON/OFF SITE

ON/OFF SITE INTRODUCTION

"Fabrication is the physical engagement of process with material. The method of manipulation, of engaging the physical and environmental practicalities: hardness, malleability, material, molecular, organisation, specific gravity, weathering, thermal properties . . . these determine the way in which one engages matter. The method of material engagement is the foundation of fabrication, relating the material to the form intrinsically."[1]

The strategy of *on/off site* is often used when it is more convenient to complete the construction of the new interior remotely to the host building. This approach usually involves the fabrication of objects, elements, rooms, or even buildings either adjacent to the host or at a distance, such as a factory, where it is then transported to the site and fitted. This ready-made approach might be undertaken for a variety of reasons, ranging from the complex condition of the site through to the availability of resources and the economics of the project.

On/off-site production is often formulated as one of two methods of construction: one-off or batch. The modularization or standardization of interior elements during batch production will usually be economically beneficial, as they can replicated and assembled with ease, as opposed to the construction of a one-off or bespoke element. In either procedure, when off-site construction takes place, the processes can usually be carefully monitored and if required the fabrication of elements can be of a very high quality. This is due to their close monitoring away from the busy and distracting building site. The on/off-site processes will also usually cut down on waste, usually making prefabricated construction highly efficient in both sustainable and ecological terms.

The construction and fabrication of elements both on and off-site during a project is a strategy that can lead to a variety of unusual interior solutions. Whether off the peg or bespoke, one-off or batch, the fabricated element can often lead to the creation of very particular and unique building reuse solutions. Ready-made elements such as shipping containers, parts of trucks, unused white goods such as fridges and washing machines, along with more traditional modular elements such as doors or windows can be assembled in unusual configurations to make useable interior spaces. This is as well as other modularized standard materials such as sheet timber, steel and timber sections and so on.

Sometimes in order to prime the site to accept the on/off-site constructed elements, conservation, preservation and restoration strategies will be utilized. This will be in order to create an idealized backdrop for the placement of the new object and the integration of the new elements into the adapted building.

Dovecote Studio
The one-story brick building was repurposed to house an artist's studio by carefully inserting a prefabricated steel house into the stabilized crumbling ruins of the old dovecote.

PROENZA SCHOULER

PROJECT

PROENZA SCHOULER

DESIGNERS

ADJAYE ASSOCIATES

LOCATION

NEW YORK CITY, USA

DATE

2012

"Building off-site leads to reduced material waste and labor costs, while the fabrication of modular or transportable elements allows for adaptability and reuse."[2]

The deployment of ready-made elements in the design of an interior can lend distinct and unusual spatial qualities to a project. Inspiration for the utilization of a ready-made element such as a particular material, form or shape, is often to be located in the context of the project, among the site, and within the clients' requirements and wishes.

Lazaro Hernandez and Jack McCollough, the founders of the fashion house Proenza Schouler, commissioned David Adjaye Associates to deliver a unique interior space for their first store in New York City. The 3,000-square-foot retail space occupies the first and second floors of a neo-Classical townhouse in a residential area of uptown Madison Avenue.

The geometric-patterned, hard-edged aesthetic of the fashion house's sumptuous garments provided the inspiration for a recurring motif used throughout the interior. After a series of experiments with the name and logo Adjaye Associates created an abstracted, geometric pattern, reminiscent of a recurring motif that is often hammered and scored into Hernandez and McCollough's garments. This prefabricated symbol is used to form the bronzed-steel front door of the retail space and the screen that partially encloses the circulation between the floors of the shop at the back of the interior. Therefore, this has ensured that an abstracted form of the fashion designers geometric sensibility and aesthetic encloses all of the transition points in the interior, intrinsically linking movement and their spatial identity.

The removal of the existing floor in the front of the historic building created a dramatic double height entrance space. In this lobby a concrete floor extends the exterior sidewalk of the city into the interior. It guides the customer away from the elevator lobby and across the space into a long thin room that is lined with aged timber columns and beams. The structure, a timber pavilion, runs the length of the space. In amongst this structure the designers placed a system of changeable shelves that display handbags, shoes and accessories. The system can be reorganized at regular intervals and can accommodate new season changes or particular collections of accessories.

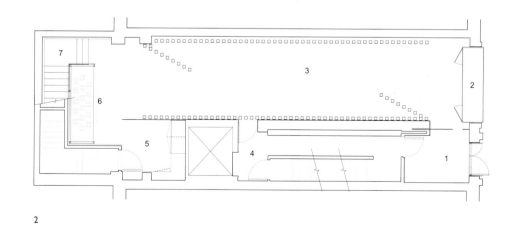

1

1 The new geometric patterned screen door discretely signals the new showroom and the identity of the fashion house in the listed façade of the building.

2 The long, thin room is simply organized.

1—ENTRY VESTIBULE
2—DISPLAY BOX
3—TIMBER PAVILION
4—ELEVATOR LOBBY
5—POINT OF SALE
6—DISPLAY
7—FEATURE STAIR

2

FIRST FLOOR

5FT   10FT   20FT   North

3

4

3 The spatial identity of the space is encapsulated in the two-story lobby and through the combination of the raw surfaces of the existing building, the timber pavilion, and the precast concrete mezzanine lining.

4 The timber joists and bronzed-steel tube rails create a raw context for the refined clothes among the precast, flecked, concrete panels.

5 The bronzed-steel, geometric-patterned screen wraps the stairs between the upper and lower floors deep in the space.

The upper mezzanine is accessed via the stair at the back of the space. A flecked pre-cast concrete panelled u-shaped section counterpoints the dark timbered cavernous first floor. Ready-to-wear items hang from bronzed-steel sales racks suspended from the ceiling. Fitting rooms are lined with sensuous sandy-colored buffalo leather.

The urban context provided the material language for the interior space. The surfaces of the existing building were primed in order to create an ideal backdrop for the new interior elements. Holes, repairs, and pieces of ad hoc masonry were left in situ as reminders of the past of the building. The exposed walls were stained with a wash that makes it appear lived in.

The combination of raw and sleek materials in this gritty urban environment creates a vibrant backdrop for the refined fashion garments.

5

CHARLES SMITH WINES

PROJECT

CHARLES SMITH WINES

DESIGNERS

OLSON KUNDIG

ARCHITECTS

LOCATION

WALLA WALLA,

WASHINGTON, USA

DATE

2012

"Another aspect of the Readymade is its lack of uniqueness . . . a point which I want very much to establish is that the choice of these 'ready-mades' was never dictated by aesthetic delectation."[3]

Sometimes the qualities of a very particular material can provide the impetus for the identity of a new interior. The choice of material, the adaptation of the context in which it will be deployed, and the way in which it is fabricated, can create a unique space where the requirements of the client are communicated in an emphatic fashion. Off-The-Peg solutions to the design of the interior can provide unique or innovative ways in which projects can be realized.

The vintner Charles Smith commissioned Olson Kundig to design a space in which to showcase his wine. The space needed to draw wine tourists from Smith's surrounding vineyards into downtown Walla Walla, in order to attend tasting based events and to sample the goods. The store needed to have a presence on the street and also contain a workspace for up to fourteen people. Smith chose the Johnson Auto Electric Building, a redundant car workshop constructed in 1917. The large single span space, free from any supporting internal columns, encouraged the designers to leave the space as open as possible, creating a fluid and flexible "event" space that was populated by a series of moveable pieces of furniture.

In contrast to the open event space, the workspace, containing an office and conference room—both requiring some moments of privacy—was enclosed. It was housed in a large rectangular volume affectionately termed the "armadillo." Placed into one-third of the three-bay garage the prefab, timber-frame room was constructed on site and slotted into the northernmost area of the garage. The workspace was named after the fifteen steel panels that cover its top and sides. The welded steel, L-shaped panels were layered over each other like the leathery armored shell of the animal they were named after. Running on tracks, each panel was able to be pulled back to open up the workspace to the event space tasting room. During events the previously private room could become a stage, ensuring that when needed it could blur the divide between the front and back of house activities.

Two of the garage's three large, front openings were remodeled with new glass and steel doors inserted into them. In a nod to the auto-industry past of the building, and to add to the theatricality of the space, the pivoted panels can be hand-cranked open, opening the garage interior to the street and providing shelter to outside drinkers.

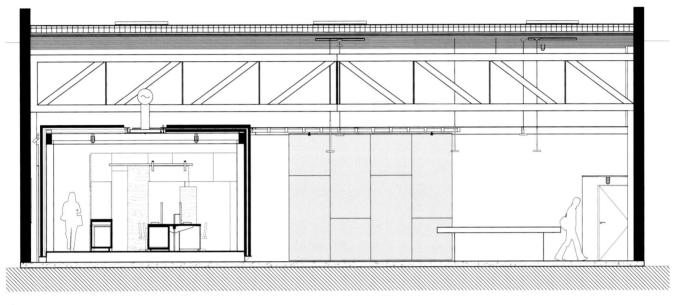

1

```
0 1 2 3 4      8        12
```

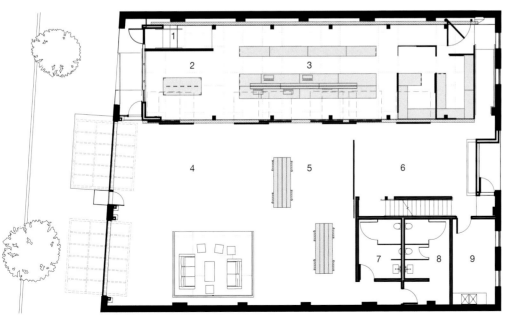

1 Huge timber trusses negate the need for internal structure and allow the garage to remain as open plan as possible.

2 The plan is organized into two main areas: the enclosed workspace and the open plan "event" tasting room.

1—ENTRY
2—CONFERENCE ROOM
3—OFFICE
4—WAREHOUSE
5—TASTING AREA
6—SERVICE AREA
7—MEN'S RESTROOM
8—WOMEN'S RESTROOM
9—STORAGE/MECHANICAL

Second Floor Plan

```
0   5   10       20
```

3 Two custom-made doors are built for the original garage openings. The third opening is kept for the entrance to the office and the warehouse.

4 The L-shaped steel panels of the "armadillo" workspace can be slid back and forth across the timber frame and can be arranged to open up the interior to the tasting room.

5 The raw, untreated surfaces of the garage are retained in order to create a backdrop for the furniture of the space as well as to act as a metaphor for the processes of wine making and time.

The raw and unfinished quality of the interior was enhanced through leaving the space bare and "as found." Treated as though a "ready-made" the designers retained previous workers' scribbles on the wall and the parking lines and markings on the concrete floor, combining them with the discolored stains on the timber trusses of the leaking roof. All of these decisions encouraged the visitor to read the spatial aesthetic as a rough-and-ready type of space. New materials added to this environment also need to communicate a patina of wear and tear through their constant use. The steel plates of the "armadillo" will discolor through time and use. The timber tops of the bar and tables will reveal their wear and tear over time and the stacked crates and boxes used to support the tasting tables will decay before being replaced. Like the processes of making fine wine, it is envisaged that this interior will also show the wear and tear of aging, resulting in a better and more mature space over the course of a long period of time.

3

4

5

DOVECOTE STUDIO

PROJECT
DOVECOTE STUDIO
DESIGNERS
HAWORTH TOMPKINS
LOCATION
SNAPE MALTINGS, UK
DATE
2009

"Most building adaptation is, like most building evolution, vernacular."[4]

An on/off-site strategy is often utilized when a design solution is required that is closely related to a place and to a specific building reuse. Yet it is usually employed when the element or module needs to be fabricated away from the site. This may be because construction space is limited, it might be cheaper to pre-fabricate, or the site to be reused is fragile and sensitive. Sometimes this approach can often result in an interior that is not *site-specific*, creating a *non-contextual* design. In this project this strategy has resulted in a space that is made explicitly a part of its context even though it has been constructed in another place. It is this counterpoint of old and new, on and off-site, that has resulted in an adaptation that looks striking and unique.

As part of the extension of the Aldeburgh Campus, at Snape Maltings Suffolk, home to the famous music festival founded by Benjamin Britten, the ruined shell of the old dovecote was repurposed in order to house a small artists' studio. Founded in 1948, the festival moved into the converted Victorian Maltings barn in 1967. Britten, with cofounder Peter Pears and Eric Crozier, set about acquiring the surrounding buildings in order to establish a center for music and musicians, developing the internationally renowned festival as well as shops, restaurants, and galleries. In 2009, the Haworth Tompkins master plan created new performance and rehearsal spaces in the numerous grade 2 listed industrial buildings across the site. The plan for the regeneration of the site included the expansion of the music campus, better landscaping, provision of a new visitor center, and construction of a musicians' café. The artist's studio completed the project within one of the most sensitive structures on site, the ruin of a dovecote.

N

0   1   5m

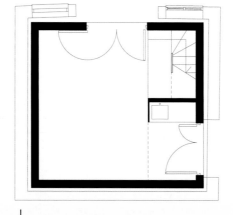
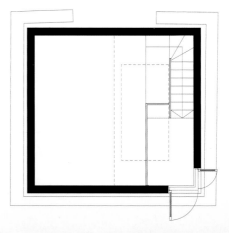

I

1 The simple studio space allows an artist to make it his or her own while in residency.

2 The new and the old are separated by a slight gap where a shallow drainage channel is placed for removing any excess water.

The one-story brick dovecote on the edge of the site had been derelict since the 1970s. Its ruined and decayed fabric, the fallen down brickwork and the rusting window grilles, had come to embody the journey of the site, one of industrial agriculture through to creative and cultural reuse. The symbolic quality of the dovecote inspired the designers to create a symbol for the campus, a building that respected the robust qualities of the existing industrial buildings but which could be adapted by using a contemporary and uncompromising architectural language.

The ruin was stabilized and some of the brickwork was repaired. Along with the ruined windows the vegetation that had enveloped the structure was left as it was found. A small drainage channel was dug inside the ruin to facilitate the run off of rainwater from both the new and old structures. The designers created a "ghost" of the form of the original shelter, a structure that could be placed into the shell of the old dovecote without compromising the shell of the ruin.

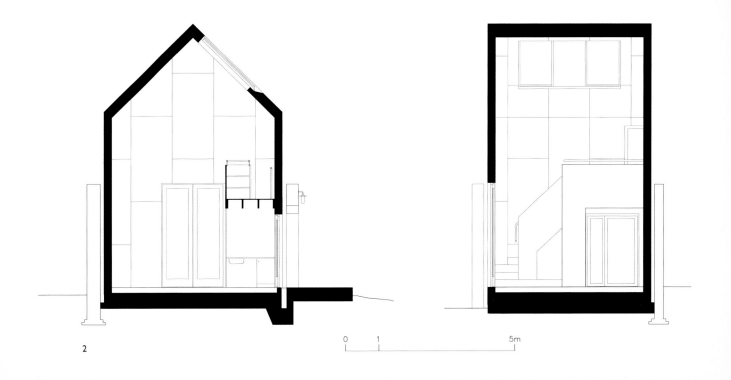

0   1   5m

3 Before adaptation, vegetation was beginning to overcome the ruined and decaying dovecote.

4 Fabricated adjacent to the ruin, the new steel studio was craned into position in one piece.

5 The two-story interior is lined with plywood and is self-contained so that the artist-in-residence can focus on his or her work.

3

4

5

The new studio was fabricated using Corten steel. Each panel was prefabricated by local steelworkers and then delivered to site to be assembled in a compound next to the brick ruin. The studio was welded together in a monocoque construction that was made like the hull of a ship, and lifted by crane, in one piece, into position. The finished Corten steel shell was placed into the ruin and ready to be occupied in just one day. The construction solved the complex challenge of working within a fragile ruin in a way that united material, structure, off-site prefabrication then delivery to site and its incorporation into the ruin. Over time the Corten steel will weather to a shade of rust-red almost exactly the same as the color of Suffolk red bricks.

The single volume will be used by artists in residence, by musicians as rehearsal or performance space, by staff for meetings, or as a temporary exhibition space. The interior walls and ceiling of the space were insulated, sealed with a high-performance vapor control layer, and lined with spruce plywood to create a timber "box" within the Corten steel shell. Laminated plywood sheets also form the stairs, balustrade, and mezzanine structures.

Internally, a large north light roof window provides even light for artists, while a small mezzanine platform with a writing desk incorporates a fully opening corner window that gives long views over the marshes toward the sea.

6 The startling contrast between the crumbling ruins of the dovecote and the sleek construction of the steel studio will be ameliorated over time as the steel and the brick colors merge.

6

OPEN AIR LIBRARY

PROJECT

OPEN AIR LIBRARY

DESIGNERS

KARO ARCHITEKTEN

LOCATION

MAGDEBURG, GERMANY

DATE

2009

"Modularity as a method is one that successfully addresses wasteful processes in design and construction. . . . The use of modular units in retrofit is both economically and ecologically beneficial."[5]

Adapting existing buildings for their reuse, as opposed to wholesale demolition, can maintain a particular link to a place. It will provide a continuity where the city, the building and the room can be combined to reinforce and retain urban character. It can also be a way of regenerating interest in run-down city centers, or places that require a kick-start in order to restore them back to health. Utilizing an on/off-site strategy for the making of a space can often involve the reuse of very particular materials with which to reinforce connections to a distinct location. It may also be a very useful way in which distinct places link communities with their environment.

An abandoned site in former East Germany where the library once stood in the center of Magdeburg, was adapted to house a small community-inspired project: a new open library. The city center had experienced an extreme shift in fortunes in the post-industrial age and as a result its urban landscape was experiencing 80 percent vacancy levels in its building stock. A new community-inspired project was needed in an attempt to arrest the urban blight. In 2005 a master plan entitled "City on Trial" was put into place. The first iteration of the plan involved the development of a new library. On the site of the old library, and with a very small budget, a 1:1 scale mock up of a possible new library building was constructed using 1,000 donated beer crates. Taking two days to stack and build, the crates were then filled with books donated by local residents. They created an open library where anybody could take a book home or stay and sit and read. The books were either returned when finished or replaced with another book, brought by the resident of the community. To encourage the community, a poetry festival was arranged and book readings were scheduled to help ensure that the project stood a good chance of success. To help the volunteers running the scheme, an adjacent empty store was used as a workshop space where community consultation could be arranged and organized.

1   2

1 The central location of the building ensured that it remained emphatically at the heart of the community.

2 The open-air library occupied a patch of wasteland in the city center of Magdeburg where the original library once stood.

The temporary beer-crate library was successful. It focused community spirit so much that the book donations kept coming; 20,000 books were rapidly accrued. Funding and donations were also given and enough money was raised to build a new, permanent library that was opened in 2009.

As well as its financial efficiency, the design and construction of the library had to be done in a way that the residents could relate to. This prompted the designers to explore an on/off-site strategy approach to the building. In 2007 KARO were aware of the demolition of a warehouse in the city of Hamm. The Horten warehouse was one of a number of retail spaces that were constructed using a particular modular tile. Designed in the 1960s by Egon Eiermann the 20 × 20-inch (50 × 50-centimeter) tile was 8 inches (20 centimeters) deep and could be constructed in a bond like a brick wall. The tile was designed as a stylized H-shape, representing Horten. Horten warehouses were present all over Germany, making it a recognizable brand and building style. Because of the demolition the tile was cheap and available in abundance. The new library was constructed on the site utilizing tiles from the demolished warehouse. A stage was added for performances and readings and a café staffed by local residents.

The new library now has 30,000 books. It is open 24 hours a day. Users do not need to register. Instead it is a "library of confidence" where the community has developed a new focus around cultural and communal events and through the emphasis on the lending of and reading of books. The main component used in the construction of the library ensured that the community could relate to this familiar element extracted from their urban environment.

3 The demolition of the Horten warehouse, in Hamm, provided an opportunity to reuse the modular block tiles from its façade and ensured the familiarity of the building's appearance to its community of users.

4 With the addition of landscaping, the open library becomes a new village green where the community can meet and socialize.

5 Apertures such as windows and bulletin boards disrupt the relentless quality of the exterior wall of the library and ensure that the tile wall is responsive to the environment in which it is placed.

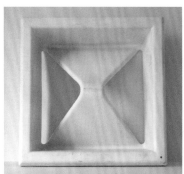

3

4

WAREHOUSE 8B

PROJECT

WAREHOUSE 8B

DESIGNERS

ARTURO FRANCO

LOCATION

MADRID, SPAIN

DATE

2011

"I prefer to think that this project emerged from opportunity, from discovering an opportunity in that rubble. In the path of exploring all the reasonable possibilities, the construction system turns into a project generator. How does that found object work? How does the flat shingle tile work? How is it stacked? How is it bonded? How do they join? These are some of the questions that arise during the processes."[6]

One important element of sustainable building practices is the reduction of energy used in the transportation of building materials to a site. Locally sourced materials are a critical component of a resourceful and responsible project build. Of equal importance in the transportation of materials to a site is the removal and responsible disposal of waste *from* the site. Innovation in both of these processes is an important aspect of an on/off-site interior strategy.

The rehabilitation of the old slaughterhouse of Madrid was a project that reworked the vast complex of buildings to house places of culture, such as a library, theater, film center, music studios, and places for creative people to meet, work, and socialize. (Also see chapter 3, Superuse.) The process of rehabilitating the buildings generated vast amounts of waste, much of it rubble, paving stones, and rotten timber, extracted from each place. In particular, each of the buildings required extensive work on their roofs, replacing the existing shingle tiles with new ones and ensuring that new insulation was applied in order to bring the spaces up to contemporary building regulations. Due to the existing buildings listed status, the new tiles had to be in accordance with the old and the rehabilitation of the old slaughterhouse buildings generated huge amounts of surplus roof tiles, many of which where stacked up inside and around a small warehouse on the edge of the site during the processes of renovation.

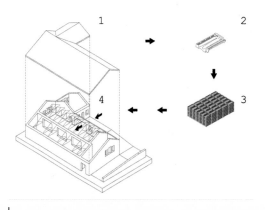

1

1 An axonometric sketch showing the processes of utilizing the roof tiles inside the building.

2 Plans and sections of the flexible space.

The municipal architect Luis Bellido designed the slaughterhouse in 1911 in a Modernist style. Warehouse 8B was constructed at the edge of the site as a storage space for the waste products of the adjacent warehouse 8. This meant that it contained the by-products of the processes of the abattoir, such as the skins of the slaughtered animals along with the salted meat, all hung out to dry in the rooms of the building.

Maintaining the supportive role of the original building in the renovation, Warehouse 8B was designated as the office space for the Matadero: the new cultural complex of the city. This administrative role was facilitated by the construction of a small office space, a flexible multifunctional presentation and reception space, and a stockroom.

The prominence of so much waste on the site prompted the designers to adopt a very simple solution to reusing the building. They reused the thousands of clay roof tiles that littered the site and which were dumped in and around the building that was to be reused. Stacked one on top of the other, and bonded with mortar, the tiles created the internal walls of the space, separating the office from the event space and enclosing the stockroom. Reclaimed timber was used to make lintels over openings such as doors in the tiled walls. When views were required, the tiles were stacked in an open bond. New floors were constructed from sheets of steel tread plate and a polished concrete floor linked the rooms. New wooden doors were constructed from reclaimed timber from the site. The space was completed with steel pendant lights.

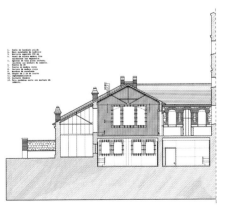

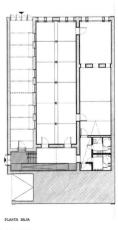

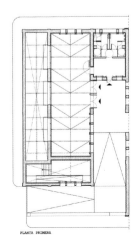

PLANTA BAJA

PLANTA PRIMERA

3 Thousands of discarded clay roof tiles waiting to be dumped littered the existing site.

4 The tiles were stacked in a different bond when light and a view was needed through the walls.

5 The unrelenting patterned quality of the stacked tile walls was offset by the monolithic, steel, tread plate flooring.

3

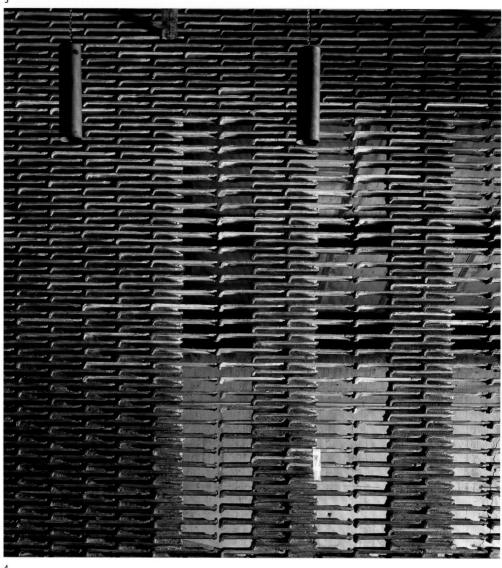

4

Notes

1. Gail Borden and Michael Meredith, *Matter, Material Processes in Architectural Production* (Oxford: Routledge, 2012), 85.

2. Deborah Schneiderman, *Inside Prefab: The Ready Made Interior* (New York: Princeton Architectural Press, 2012), 25.

3. Marcel Duchamp, "Apropos of Ready-mades" 1961. Cited in David Evans (Ed), "Appropriation." (London: Whitechapel Gallery Press, 1961), 40.

4. Stewart Brand, *How Buildings Learn – What Happens After They Are Built?* (Middlesex: Penguin Books, 1994), 156.

5. Wong Liliane "Sustainability: Industry Standards and Innovation." In Sylvia Leydecker (Ed), *Designing Interior Architecture: Concept, Typology, Material, Construction* (Basel: Birkhauser, 2013), 81.

6. Arturo Franco in conversation via materials sent to the author May 2015.

8
INSERTION

INSERTION INTRODUCTION

"*Although the inserted element is independent, particular qualities are derived from the original building. This is inevitable because the insertion always has a direct architectural relationship with the absolute physical properties of the existing space. It is built to fit.*"[1]

Insertion is a strategy that is used when a building that is to be adapted for a new use requires some kind of auxiliary construction. In general, old buildings do not always fulfil contemporary requirements for comfort, space, new functions, and technical requirements. Therefore, if they are not to be demolished, their adaptation will require new elements that will provide new spaces for differing forms of occupation, as well as the upgrade and modernization of the buildings' services and technical standards.

When using the strategy of insertion for this type of change, the inserted interior will be placed inside, in-between, on top of, around, upon, and under an existing space. Essentially inserted interiors are interior or exterior constructions that are built to fit. The host space will often dictate the form and size of the new insertion but the new element(s) will be deliberately designed to contrast with the environment in which they are placed.

The creation of interior space through the placement of elements that are built-to-fit creates a resonance between the old and the new elements. On a simple level, they will often contain particular functions, uses that the building lacked before its adaptation. These might be services, such as bathrooms or storage spaces, or elements containing new circulation, such as stairs, elevators, or ramps: all elements that are often subject to changes in regulations and technical requirements. Other insertions will contain less prosaic elements of the interior and will be designed as a main feature of the space that is to be adapted. These might be a new theater auditorium, or an addition containing an exhibition. Whichever uses the insertion contains, it will often reinvigorate the building both through its functional or technical upgrade and through the dramatic resonance of a new element being placed inside, around, underneath, on top of, or alongside a chronologically and stylistically different building.

Medialab-Prado
The old sawmill in the center of
Madrid was remodeled in order
to house the new media lab. The
concrete frame was stripped back and
a dynamic new block of services and
stairs was inserted among the rigidly
orthogonal structure.

NYU DEPARTMENT OF PHILOSOPHY

PROJECT

NYU DEPARTMENT OF PHILOSOPHY

DESIGNERS

STEVEN HOLL ARCHITECTS

LOCATION

NEW YORK CITY, USA

DATE

2007

"Working on an existing building means coming to terms with it; such work involves juggling constraints additional to those arising from the program and from building regulations. These new stimulants also act as a stimulus to the imagination; they enable architectural solutions to be developed which would never have been invented from scratch."[2]

Insertion is a strategy that can be utilized to create distinctive elements for the more pragmatic requirements of a project. Far from being merely the logistical aspects of building reuse, the new program, building regulations, circulation elements such as stairs, and access and health and safety considerations such as fire egress, can be the stimulants for an inspirational design.

The New York University Department of Philosophy commissioned Steven Holl to adapt a late nineteenth-century, six-story historic building to house faculty and graduate offices, a periodic library, classrooms, social spaces for the students, and a 120-seat auditorium. The exterior of the building was left unaltered, while the interior was reorganized around the imposing cast-iron column frame structure. The upper five floors of the building accommodated much of the cellular office-based requirements of the program, such as graduate and faculty members' offices. Each floor was arranged with the offices and seminar rooms at the periphery, maximizing the windows, natural light, and the view back across the adjacent Washington Square Park. This organization ensured that a breakout reception space was located centrally to each of the floors, which needed natural light.

Two areas key to the building's successful functioning were the auditorium and the stairs. The auditorium was placed on the first floor adjacent to the lobby. Its prominent position ensured that it was not only easily accessible but also signalled one of the vital aspects of the faculty—the communication of ideas. The organic-shaped space absorbed the columns of the first floor into its structure. The exterior was wrapped in a series of perforated patterned timber sheets.

1 An early concept sketch of the stairwell initiated the idea of a vertically connected lit space.

2 The intricacy of the perforated screens and balustrades are counterpointed by the carefully considered arrangement of the stairs in the confined space.

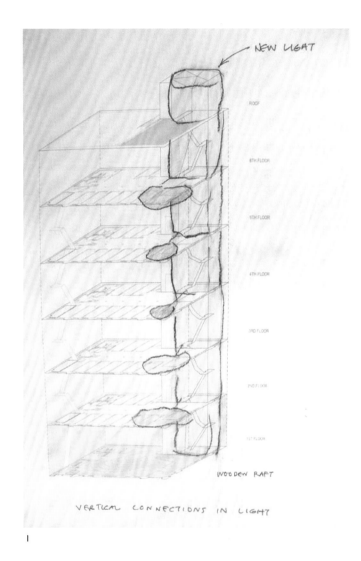

1

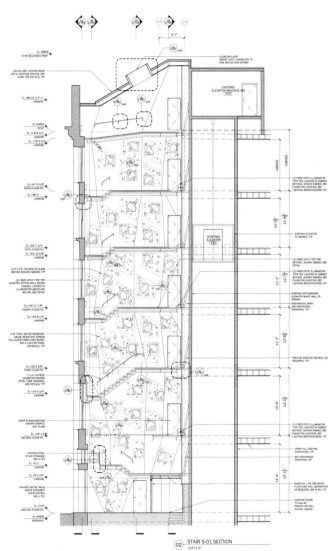

2

3

3 The exterior of the historic 1890 building remained unaltered.

4 Cube-shaped wooden seats, designed by Brent Comber, are arranged in the ground-level, cork-floored lobby adjacent to the new stairwell.

The project's most distinctive feature was the newly inserted staircase. Designed to link all of the floors of the building, the twisting stair was positioned to encourage faculty members to utilize the space and to increase social interaction. The roof at the top of the stair was open, and a new skylight was inserted in order to increase the natural light entering the vertical shaft. The surfaces of the existing building were left as found and painted white to increase the light reflections. Prismatic film was applied to some of the windows, increasing refraction and introducing a dynamic chromatic light aspect that changed as the sun moved around the southeast corner of the building where the stair was located. This effect was enhanced by the white walls of the void. Inside this vertical shaft a new steel staircase was designed to connect each floor. The painted white steel and pale concrete stepped stair twisted and turned through the enclosed void, delivering students to a large landing on each floor of the building. The balustrade was fashioned from steel plate and was perforated at irregular intervals. Akin to small sunspots, the openings added to the prismatic qualities of light passing through the void. In order to satisfy the building regulations, on each floor the stairwell was enclosed and sealed with a fire door. But rather than make a mundane enclosed screen, for the corner of every level, the enclosing screen was punctured with sunspot ovals, similar to the balustrade. The designers created a light well in the corner of every floor level, illuminating the central breakout space as well as providing an invitation for everybody to take the stair once their class or meeting was over.

The new stairwell created a vertical meeting room that joined the six-level building in a shifting and fluid, seasonally changing beam of light and shadow.

5 On each floor level the stairwell created a light source for the central breakout and socializing spaces, as well as an inviting illuminated invitation to take the stairs.

6 Large landings in the dynamic, chromatic, light-filtered stairwell encourage students and faculty to stop and interact.

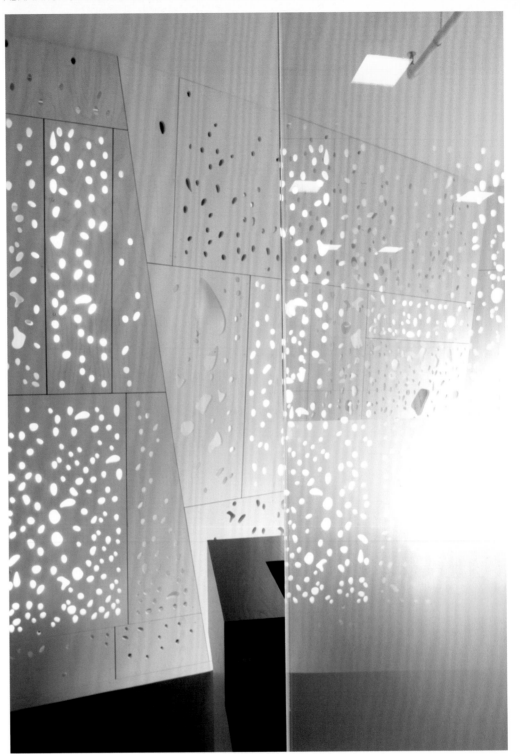

5

HOSTEL GOLLY & BOSSY

PROJECT
HOSTEL GOLLY & BOSSY
DESIGNERS
STUDIO UP
LOCATION
SPLIT, CROATIA
DATE
2010

"The converted building is always characterized by a complexity and ambiguity in terms of material, time and content; many elements are already in place and must simply be absorbed or integrated. What is required is less an ability to invent, than one to reassign and interpret."[3]

All buildings change over time. Some will be altered much faster than others and those that cannot be usefully altered will often fall into disrepair and ultimately become obsolete. Therefore, a building's adaptability is a feature that ultimately keeps it in use and fit for its purpose. Insertion is a strategy that is often used to adapt buildings by adding elements that they might be missing. Extra space such as new rooms, and services such as circulation systems or bathrooms, can be inserted into, onto, around, beside, and on top of existing buildings in order to keep them in use and ensure that they remain habitable.

Located in the center of Split, the Savo building has a long history of change of use. Each successive adaptation has altered the building irrevocably, to the point where only the façade gives any clues to its early twentieth-century Secessionist style. Originally the building was the Grand Uzor fabric store, then in 1991 the building was turned into a shopping mall. Next it was to become a large youth hostel, attracting a design conscious clientele, looking for a new experience when they stayed in the city.

Studio UP analyzed the existing building in order to examine if it could be adapted for its new use. With a limited budget, a key strategy decision was made to absorb the main elements of the existing building. The central core was retained and integrated into the project as the main circulation for the new hostel. The shopping mall escalators, panoramic elevator, and the staircase were usefully placed in the center of the building and were able to be reassigned as the main core of circulation. The remaining former shopping floor spaces were partitioned with a system of walls that were inserted into the building and which contained everything necessary for the new function.

1 The central core and the formal, early-twentieth-century exterior of the former shopping mall were all that was left of the original building.

1

2

3

4

5

2 Along with overscaled graphics the vibrant yellow circulation core of the hostel was designed to appeal particularly to a young, design conscious demographic of hostel guest.

3 The fourth-floor rooms were carefully inserted into the loft space of the existing building.

4 The relentless interior corridors of the capsule hotel dormitory rooms were overlaid with the use of bold colors and bright graphics, along with a window at the end that overlooked the city.

5 The thick walls of each dormitory contain the beds as well as storage, sinks, and bathrooms.

6 The façade and core of the building were retained and the new hostel elements were inserted around and in-between them.

The second floor was designed to accommodate a number of dormitories with up to eight beds in each. Arranged in long thin corridors, or blocks, accessed from the central core of circulation, each dormitory was designed to be reminiscent of a Japanese capsule hotel. They included a row of beds, recessed into the thick wall, with privacy curtains, light, and power sockets. The thick wall contained all services and storage and included the bathroom. While appearing cramped, the dormitories were simple and practical. Their insularity was relieved by a window placed at the end of each central corridor that gave a view to the city beyond. The third floor mixed dormitories with single rooms, while the fourth floor inserted a number of two-bed rooms into the loft space of the building.

The mostly white rooms of the hostel were counterpointed with a vibrant yellow color for the public spaces. These circulation elements were overlaid with distinctive graphics that signal directions in the interior, while contrasting the formal and austere tone of the outside of the old building.

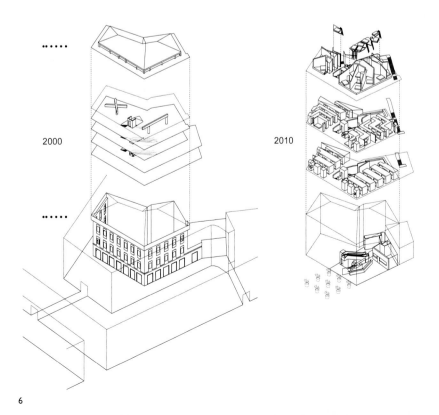

2000

2010

6

RIJKSMUSEUM

PROJECT
RIJKSMUSEUM
DESIGNERS
CRUZ Y ORTIZ
LOCATION
AMSTERDAM, NETHERLANDS
DATE
2013

"Insertion is a practice that establishes an intense relationship between the original building and the remodelling and yet allows the character of each to exist in a strong and independent manner."[4]

Insertion can be used to reinvigorate an important historic building. It can be used as a strategy for instigating a set of processes that provoke an intense and objective reassessment of the host building. New elements can be inserted into the space that will then instigate dialogue and offer clarification of the host space particularly when it has lost some of its original meaning. This can be achieved through emphasizing the dialectical relationship between both the new and the old elements of the project.

In its current location for 130 years, the Rijksmuseum had become unwelcoming and difficult to navigate. As new addition after new addition of gallery spaces and services were added over the years, with little sense of a master plan to guide them, the building lost its character. It had become a poorly lit, illogical, and inhospitable place for museumgoers to view the world-renowned collection of Dutch masters, including Rembrandt's most famous painting *The Night Watch*.

Designed in 1885 by Pierre Cuypers, the building was an orthogonally planned set of wings surrounding two courtyards. It was completed with a central on-axis entrance that separated the building into two equal parts. Designed in a hybrid, red brick and stone, neo-Gothic Renaissance style the building was originally poorly received, deemed as being too medieval. Over the years, as more space was required, the courtyards became filled with galleries, adding to the challenge of exploring the interior without getting lost.

1. INFORMATION DESK
2. TICKET DESK
3. CLOAKROOM
4. ENTRANCE TO GALLERIES
5. MUSEUM SHOP
6. TOILETS

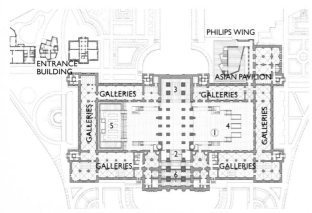

1

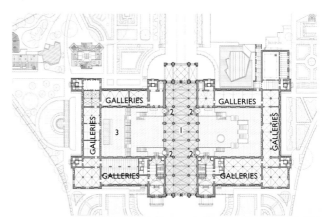

1. MUSEUM PASSAGEWAY
2. ENTRANCE TO RIJKSMUSEUM
3. CAFÉ

2

1 First floor plan. The central passageway from the north to the south of the city was maintained in the renovation.

2 Second floor plan. The galleries are arranged around the central courtyard.

3 Section. The new square was excavated from the basement. A 30-foot (9-meter) deep subterranean auditorium and retail space created an extra engineering challenge, which was to keep the basement dry in the below sea-level Dutch landscape.

Since 2003, in a ten-year renovation, the designers reinvigorated the building by clarifying its original plan and reinstating a logical progression through the galleries. They did this by clearing out the infill of the courtyards and enclosing them with new roofs and inserting an enormous new public square at the center of the building. The designers also restored the original gallery rooms, reinstating the vibrant colors of the original building, with their various nuances of grays and blues, which had been lost to the repeated whitewashing of the walls, since the 1920s. Informing some of these decisions was the fact that the central spine of the museum had always been a public passageway, allowing citizens to pass through the museum from the north to the south of the city without stepping inside the galleries. An earlier iteration of the project was abandoned after protests that the passageway was to be relocated. Instead Cruz y Ortiz maintained the public right of way and excavated the courtyards underneath the route. This linked both sides of the building at a subterranean level with a new basement public square. They contained the main entrance, ticket desk, cloakroom, shop, café, and entrance to the galleries.

1. MUSEUM PASSAGEWAY
2. ENTRANCE TO RIJKSMUSEUM
3. ENTRANCE TO GALLERIES
4. AUDITORIUM
5. MUSEUM SHOP
6. CAFÉ

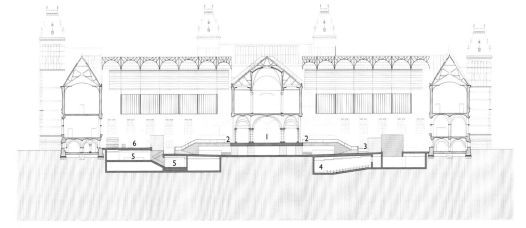

3

4 The newly renovated library.

5 The excavated courtyard created a new public square for the building. It linked both sides of the museum and maintained the public route through the middle of the building. The new chandelier created a human scale to the space while controlling the acoustics and the lighting of the atria.

6 The renovation revealed the original colors of the galleries, which had been covered over by successive layers of whitewash to create a neutral backdrop.

The courtyards were also designed to act as giant light sources for the rest of the galleries. The designers fitted the atria-like spaces with huge cage-like chandeliers that acted as sound baffles as well as providing artificial lighting.

The designers completed the courtyard with a simple palette of limestone, designed to reflect the brightly lit monochromatic courtyards. The newly restored galleries and their entrances were in direct contrast to the simplicity of the courtyard and their rich colors and materials ensured a stark contrast between the new and the old of the museum. To complement this contrast the exhibition and lighting designer assembled both paintings and objects together in the galleries. This ensured that paintings were arranged with contemporary suits of armour, ceramics, and textiles all from the same period as the image. Discreet indirect lighting illuminated each room. The only object that remained on display during the renovation and which was returned to its original location where it was installed in 1885 was Rembrandt's *The Night Watch.* This gesture completed the circuitous dialogue between the new and the old in the museum's rehabilitation.

4

5

6

CARRER AVINYÓ

PROJECT

CARRER AVINYÓ

DESIGNERS

DAVID KOHN ARCHITECTS

LOCATION

BARCELONA, SPAIN

DATE

2013

"Numerous architects have tackled the problem of inserting new uses into large existing spaces by taking a 'house-in-house' approach, in which the new use is more or less independent from the existing construction."[6]

The balance between public and private spaces in a domestic interior needs careful consideration. While often insular, and designed to be a safe and secure environment protecting its inhabitants from the outside world, domestic space can be closely connected to the city in which it resides. Insertion can be utilized as a method of enhancing and distinguishing, as well as sometimes rendering ambiguous, the boundaries between what is public domestic space and what is the private interior.

In a nineteenth-century apartment block, where Carrer d'Escudellers joins Carrer d'Avinyo, in the Gothic quarter of Barcelona, David Kohn was commissioned to adapt an existing second-floor apartment into a new home. In this part of old Barcelona the city grid fragments into a more erratic pattern. The location and shape of the host building ensured that the plan of the apartment building had a distinctive triangular form—one that is echoed in the adjacent public space, Plaça George Orwell.

The demolition of a series of subdividing walls in the apartment opened the space into one large, 16-foot (5-meter) high, angular, single room. Four large floor-to-ceiling windows, each with balconies, flooded the room with natural light and connected the interior back into the city. Kohn designed the large room to be a public space, with a domestic interior, that was a living, dining, socializing room where the clients and their guests could feel as though they were a part of the city. To reinforce this connection, Kohn designed a new floor. The mosaic floor of the apartment was decorated with a triangular pattern that matched the geometry of the plan: a tactic that reinforced the interior's connection to the city. The tile pattern was gradated in color from green at one end of the apartment to red at the other in order to differentiate the client's private spaces.

1 The plan of the lower level of the apartment.

2 An axonometric drawing depicting the space with the upper balcony level clearly visible.

1—BEDROOM
2—ENTRANCE LOBBY
3—SHOWER ROOM
4—UTILITY ROOM
5—LIVING ROOM
6—KITCHEN

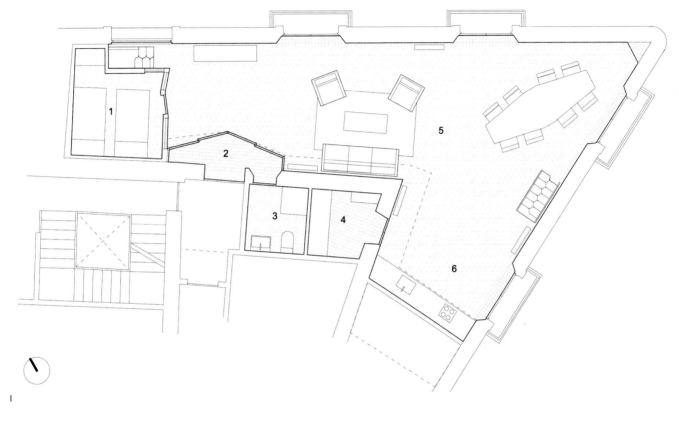

1

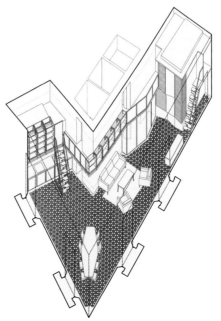

2

3

In order to re-establish the private aspects of the domestic interior, lost in the previous demolition of the subdividing walls, a two-story piece of furniture was inserted into the far end of the room. This "house-within-a-house" contained two bedrooms stacked one on top of the other. The furniture was given the appearance of a small building—at this point convoluting the relationship between the interior and the city. The journey from public social space to the private interior of the bedroom was completed by closing the louvers of the façade of the furniture element, ensuring that the bedroom became separated from the main socializing space.

A high-level library balcony was designed to connect each of the upper level bedrooms to their en suite bathrooms. A large, specially designed angular dining table was placed at the street corner where the red and green tiles mixed. Its location was significant in that it provided a subtle invitation to the clients and their guests to gather, often around some food, and socialize in the space and join together where the public and the private both meet.

3 The apartment occupies the second floor of the angular building on the corner of Carrer d'Avinyo and Carrer d'Escudellers.

4 The entrance to the living room of the apartment was placed directly underneath an angular landing of the balcony. Access to the main room is through a glass screen that separates the communal stair from the interior. The two-story bedroom furniture was positioned to the right.

5 The 16-foot (5-meter) high room is flooded with natural light from four balconied floor-to-ceiling windows. The library balcony links the upper level of the apartment bedrooms with the bathroom.

4

5

6 The second inserted element of furniture contained the kitchen and the library as well as balcony access to the other bedroom and bathrooms.

7 The strategic positioning of the dining table in the corner of the room is a constant and inviting reminder of the social dimension of the public role of the interior space.

MEDIALAB-PRADO

PROJECT

MEDIALAB-PRADO

DESIGNERS

LANGARITA-NAVARRO

ARQUITECTOS

LOCATION

MADRID, SPAIN

DATE

2013

"There is nothing new about buildings changing their function. Because structure tends to outlive function, buildings throughout history have been adapted to all sorts of new uses."[7]

Not all aspects of a building change throughout time. The way that they are utilized by their occupants will often change, and the building will adapt accordingly. The perception of a building will change and how it is perceived or regarded in its context will evolve over time. In contrast to this, and bar minor adaptations to facilitate new use, the structural elements of a building will often remain static and intact. This is for a number of reasons, but it is primarily for economic motives, as the structure of a building is often one of the more difficult and expensive aspects of a building to drastically alter. Therefore, a number of particular structural systems will lend themselves to their remodelling using the strategy of insertion. The provision of elements that are built to fit a particular form, governed by its structure and envelope, will often result in a dynamic juxtaposition between both the new and old components of the building.

In 2008, La Serreria Belga, the Belgian Sawmill, was the focus of an architectural competition to remodel it to become the Medialab-Prado. The old sawmill was one of very few examples of industrial architecture still surviving in central Madrid. It was built over a number of phases during the 1920's by the architect Manuel Álvarez Naya, and was one of the first architectural examples in Madrid to use exposed reinforced concrete. In the competition it was stipulated that these distinguishing features should be retained in the new project.

Named because of its proximity to the Prado Museum, Medialab-Prado is a part of the Department of Arts, Sports and Tourism of Madrid City Council. The lab was conceived as a space for the production, research and dissemination of cultural projects that explore collaborative forms of experimentation and learning that are emerging from digital networks and new technologies. The 43,000 square feet (4000 square meters) of the existing building were to be redesigned to accommodate workshops, open labs, meeting spaces and conferences. All of these were to be enclosed in a building that was to have a new three-story high digital façade: a screen that would transmit the work of the occupants to the adjacent busy Plaza de las Letras.

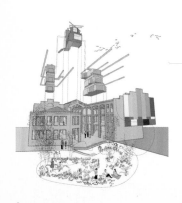

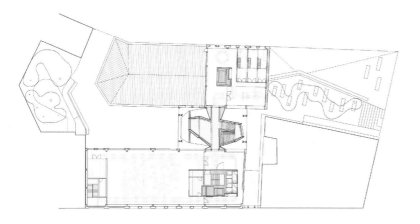

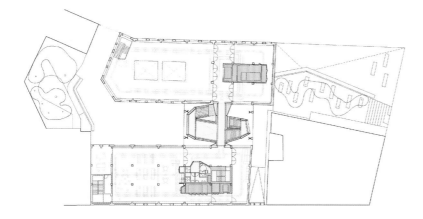

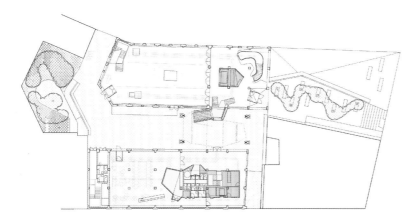

1   While elements are often built to fit their new host space, the strategy of insertion ensures that new objects inside an old space can sometimes appear quite distinct and look as though they have been parachuted into place.

2/4   New elements containing bathrooms were placed in each of the two wings. The consolidation of these services allowed each floor to remain open and flexible for a variety of uses.

2

3

4

5 The "thing" is represented as a translucent, lightweight, three-story circulation tower inserted into the concrete frame of the link between the two wings of the existing building.

6 The rough and ready concrete frame and floors of the existing building are retained, maintaining the industrial character of the place.

7 The ethereal atmosphere of the interior was designed to ensure that there was a stark contrast between the exposed concrete of the two wings of the sawmill that the new space now connected.

5

6

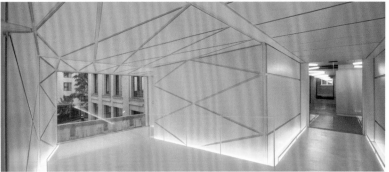

7

Langarita Navarro won the competition and facilitated the new use of the building by inserting a new circulation element that slotted into a stripped back concrete frame between the two wings of the old industrial building. Nicknamed "the thing", the new inserted element contained circulation as well as break out spaces with which to facilitate the open and flexible spatial requirements of the new use. The three-story volume was inserted into a void at the center of the old sawmill, and was designed to stand out as a new sculptural element in contrast to the rigid formality of the concrete frame structure around it. The "thing" was constructed from lightweight panels and featured translucent walls that could be illuminated with different neon colors. With one eye on a possible future transformation of the building, the lightweight module could also be disassembled and the building remodeled for a different use at another time.

The lightweight, glowing structure radically contrasted with the concrete frame of the host building. A lighter touch was applied to the two adjacent wings that were designed to house the main facilities of the lab. The existing concrete structure was cleaned and any new insertions, such as services, were placed inside timber boxes constructed as a tower in both wings. The stark contrast between the existing buildings' concrete frame and structure and the crisp new insertions ensured that the relationship between the new and old components of the remodeling was clearly delineated.

Notes

1. Graeme Brooker and Sally Stone, *Rereadings-Interior Architecture and The Principles of Remodelling Existing Buildings* (London: Riba-Enterprises, 2004), 102.

2. Robert, Philippe, *Adaptations. New Uses for Old Buildings* (New York: Princeton, 1989), 5.

3. Christian Schittich, *Building in Existing Fabric: Refurbishment, Extension, New Design* (Basel: Birkhauser, 2004), 20.

4. Graeme Brooker and Sally Stone, *Rereadings-Interior Architecture and The Principles of Remodelling Existing Buildings* (London: Riba-Enterprises, 2004), 102.

5. Ibid.

6. Johannes Cramer and Stefan Breitling, *Architecture in Existing Fabric* (Birkhauser, 2007), 120.

7. Sherban Cantacuzino, *Re/Architecture. Old Buildings New Uses* (London: Thames & Hudson, 1989), 8.

ACCRETIONS
Describes the accumulation or growth of layer upon layer of matter. In old buildings the stripping back and analysis of these layers can prove influential in the building's reuse.

ADAPTATION
The process of transforming an existing element or building in order for it to accommodate a new use or appearance.

APPLIED TEXTURE
Added material, such as metal, fabric, plastic, or timber, that can be applied to an existing surface in order to create or shape the new visual and atmospheric identity of an interior.

APPROPRIATION
The adoption or use of an element such as a building for uses other than it may have been intended for.

ARTIFICE
Designers sometimes employ devices or particular maneuvers that are meant to deceive or to trick the viewer into thinking they are looking at something else. False perspectives, exaggerated or unusually scaled details, or materials that mimic other finishes are examples of artifice in an interior.

CIRCULATION
The methods of movement within a building. Circulation is often arranged as a series of horizontal routes through a building via walkways, corridors, and bridges, or vertically via stairs, ramps, elevators, and escalators.

CLADDING
The application of a layer of material that covers the structure of a building or element. On the outside of a building this may have to consider weathering and climate control. In an interior, cladding is more important in terms of performance, look, and identity. The relationship between cladding and structure is a complex issue that dominates architectural and design history.

COLLAGE
Refers to the assemblage of a series of fragments usually, but not exclusively, cut out from magazines, newspapers, and books, to be formed into a new image with different meanings. Can also be applied to buildings formed from different parts. *See also* Spolia.

COMPOSITION
The plan or arrangement of elements in a visual design. In interior planning composition relates to the organization of the components of space. In elevations or sections, composition can relate to the deployment of rooms and interior elements in the building.

CONCEPT
Will often be an idea, scheme, or initiative that is used to provide an abstract or more pragmatic guide for the progress and process of a design project.

CONCRETE
A solid, composite material formed from aggregate bonded with cement and water. It can be poured on site, usually in a mold or shuttering, or precast. Across larger expanses, it is usually reinforced with steel.

CONSERVATION
The art of conserving existing structures in their present form or returning them back to their original state.

CONTEXT
The conditions surrounding the building that is to be reused. These conditions may be in close proximity or far away and have a variety of impacts upon the new interior.

COUNTERPOINT
Spatial counterpoints are used to transform space through the deliberate position of opposite forms, elements, and materials in close proximity to each other.

DETAIL
The finalizing of a space and the application of materials and surfaces to an interior scheme is known as "detailing." This often involves joinery, the application of materials, and sometimes prototyping through mock-ups and samples.

ELEVATION
Usually a drawing of an outside wall or a façade of a building that shows windows, doors, and other details.

ENFILADE
Refers to a group of rooms formally aligned with each other, usually through an adjoining doorway.

ENVIRONMENT
Refers to the context of a building, as well as climatic issues in the design of interior spaces.

FORM
The basic shape of any element.

FOUND TEXTURE
When working with existing buildings, surfaces within the space can be retained and used to provide meaningful connections to the original site.

FUNCTION
The use of space within a building is often referred to as "function." *See also* Occupation.

INSERTION

An insertion-based strategy consists of the placement of an independent element or structure in, on top off, beside, around, or underneath an existing building.

INSTALLATION

The placement of a single or a series of elements into an existing building in such a way as to not substantially affect the existing building when the elements are removed. An installation might also be temporal.

INTERIOR ARCHITECTURE

Interior architecture refers to the practice of remodeling existing buildings. As well as the robust reworking of a building interior, interior architecture often deals with complex structural, environmental, and servicing problems. Interior architecture is sometimes referred to as adaptation, adaptive reuse, or remodeling.

INTERIOR DECORATION

Interior decoration is the art of decorating inside spaces and rooms to impart a particular character and atmosphere to the room. It is often concerned with such issues as surface pattern, ornamentation, furniture, soft furnishings, and lighting.

INTERIOR DESIGN

Interior design is an interdisciplinary practice that is concerned with the creation of a range of interior environments that articulate identity and atmosphere through the manipulation of spatial volume, the placement of specific objects and furniture, and the treatment of surfaces.

INTERVENTION

When a building is reused in such a way that the new and old become intertwined and reliant on each other then it is considered to be an intervention.

LOAD BEARING

Elements that absorb or carry a weight in a building, and which are difficult to remove without any significant structural changes, are considered to be load bearing.

MONUMENT

Usually refers to a structure that has been designed to commemorate a significant event or person. When something is considered "monumental" it is usually an element that is large scaled.

NARRATIVE

A narrative is a story or a text that describes a sequence of characters and events. In architecture and design, narrative is used to describe the stories or the sequence of events that the designer wishes to convey: whether an existing building, an exhibition design, or the concept or brand identity of a space.

OBJECT

A purposefully placed object is one that is loaded with meaning. Whether the object is a small piece of furniture, a large sculpture, or a number of pieces clustered together it establishes a physical and cultural relationship with its environment.

OCCUPATION

When an existing building is inhabited with a new use it can be referred to as being occupied. *See also* Function.

OFF SITE

The construction of an object or element that is away from the place in which it will reside is referred to as "off site."

ON SITE

Describes the fabrication of an entity that is undertaken on the location within which it is to be situated.

ORGANIZATION

Organization can be described as the planning or arrangement of a space; that is, the objects, rooms, and elements.

ORNAMENT

An ornament is a decorative detail than can be used to embellish parts of a building or an interior. It is often superfluous and it became a highly contested element of design in the twentieth century.

POSTPRODUCTION

The addition of special effects at the end of the filmmaking process.

READY-MADE

The development of art from utilitarian, everyday, found objects not normally considered to be art. The term *ready-made* was coined by the artist Marcel Duchamp who created a series of objet d'art from such ready-made items as a bicycle wheel, a bottle rack, and a urinal.

REFURBISHED

Originally referring to being "polished," to *furbish* something means to give it a new lease on life through its renovation.

REGENERATION

The renewal of an entity, such as an area of a city, through economic, infrastructural, and built environment investment and redevelopment.

REMODELING

The process of wholeheartedly altering a building's use, structure, identity, and appearance.

RENOVATION

Renovation is the process of renewing and updating a building. The function will remain the same and the structure is generally untouched, but the manner in which the building is used will be brought up to date. It is usually the services that require attention, especially the heating and sanitary systems.

REPROGRAMMING

Changing the use of a building through designing a new use for it.

REUSE

The transformation of an existing building will often incorporate the combination of various old and new elements in order to create something contemporary and up-to-date. See also Interior Architecture, Remodeling.

SECTION

At any point on the plan of a building, the designer may describe a line through the drawing and visualize a vertical cut through the spaces. This is called a "section"; it will explain the volumes of the spaces and indicate the position of the walls, the floors, the roof, and other structural elements.

SITE-SPECIFIC

The site is the specific location or context of a building or space. "Site-specific" is a term used to describe the influences that are derived directly from the particular conditions found on site.

SPOLIA

Derived from "spoils of war," Spolia describes the act of appropriating building elements and applying them to new or later monuments. See also Collage.

STRATEGY

An approach, methodology, instrument, or device used to implement and organize spatial changes.

STRUCTURE

A shelter or an enclosure that distinguishes inside and outside space. Structure is one of the basic elements of the construction of space and usually takes the form of materials assembled in such a way as to withstand the pressures put upon them.

SUPERUSE

A phrase formulated by 2012Architecten in the Netherlands to describe environments that are predominantly formulated by recycling elements located through the development of a harvest map.

SUSTAINABILITY

In the built environment, the sensible use of natural materials and resources in the construction industry needs to be approached in a sustainable fashion in order not to deplete natural resources and contribute further to climate change and environmental damage.

SYNTAX

Describes a set of rules defining the structure of a design language or of the organizing principles of a building.

THRESHOLD

The threshold is the point of transition between two spaces, whether this is inside and outside or two interior spaces.

TRUNKING

A rigid or flexible conduit that is often made from plastic, or sometimes steel, that contains wires and cabling discretely when fixed to a wall, floor, or ceiling.

BOOKS

Bloszies, Charles. *Old Buildings, New Designs*. New York: Princeton Architectural Press, 2011.

Bonnemaison, Sarah and Ronit Eisenbach. *Installations By Architects—Experiments in Building and Design*. New York: Princeton Architectural Press, 2011.

Borden, Gail and Michael Meredith. *Matter, Material Processes in Architectural Production*. Oxford: Routledge, 2012.

Bourriaud, Nicholas. *Postproduction*. New York: Lukas & Steinberg, 2002.

Brand, Stewart. *How Buildings Learn—What Happens After They Are Built?* Middlesex: Penguin Books, 1994.

Brilliant, Richard and Dale Kinney. *Reuse Value Spolia and Appropriation in Art and Architecture from Constantine to Sherrie Levine*. Chichester: Ashgate,2011.

Brooker, Graeme. *Key Interiors Since 1900*. London: Laurence King, 2013.

Brooker, Graeme and Lois Weinthal. *The Handbook of Interior Architecture & Design*. London: Bloomsbury, 2013.

Brooker, Graeme and Sally Stone. *From Organisation to Decoration: An Interiors Reader*. Oxon: Routledge, 2013.

Brooker, Graeme and Sally Stone. *Rereadings-Interior Architecture and The Principles of Remodelling Existing Buildings*. London: Riba-Enterprises, 2004.

Cantacuzino, Sherban. *Re/Architecture. Old Buildings New Uses*. London: Thames & Hudson, 1989.

Ciorra, Pippo and Sara Marini. *RE-CYCLE. Strategies for Architecture, City and Planet*. Milan: Electa, 2012.

Coates, Nigel. *Narrative Architecture*. Chichester: Wiley-Academy, 2012.

Colomina, Beatriz. *Privacy & Publicity. Modern Architecture as Mass Media*. Boston: MIT Press, 1996.

Colomina, Beatriz. *Sexuality & Space*. New York: Princeton Architectural Press, 1992.

Cramer, Johannes and Stefan Breitling. *Architecture in Existing Fabric*. Basel: Birkhauser, 2007.

David, Joshua and Robert Hammond. *High Line: The Inside Story of New York City's Park In The Sky*. New York: Farrar, Strauss and Giroux, 2011.

Dernie, David. *Exhibition Design*. London: Laurence King, 2006.

Douglas, James. *Building Adaptation*. Oxford: Butterworth Heinemann, 2006.

Edwards, Clive. *Interior Design—A Critical Introduction*. BERG, 2011.

Evans, David (Eds) (2009) "Appropriation" Whitechapel Gallery Press.

Fernandez Per, Aurora and Javier Mozas. *Reclaim, Remediate, Reuse, Recycle*. Spain: A+T Publishers, 2012.

Flood, Catherine and Gavin Grindon. *Disobedient Objects*. London: V&A publishing, 2014.

Forty, Adrian. *Words & Buildings: A Vocabulary of Modern Architecture*. London: Thames & Hudson, 2012.

Fuss, Diana. *The Sense of An Interior—Four Writers and the Rooms That Shaped Them*. New York: Routledge, 2004.

Hegewald, Julia and Subrata Mitra. *Re-Use. The Art and Politics of Integration and Anxiety*. London: 2012.

Hill, Jonathan. *Occupying Architecture*. Oxon: Routledge, 1998.

Hinte, Ed van, Peeren, Cesare & Jongert, Jan. *Superuse*. Netherlands: 010 Publishers, 2007.

Koolhaas, Rem. *Elements*, New York: Rizzoli, 2014.

Leydecker, Sylvia. *Designing Interior Architecture. Concept, Typology, Material, Construction*. Basel: Birkhauser, 2013.

Littlefield, David and Saskia Lewis. *Architectural Voices. Listening To Old Buildings*. London: Wiley-Academy, 2007.

Massey, Anne. *Interior Design Since 1900*. London: Thames and Hudson, 2008.

Muir, Peter. *Gordon Matta-Clark's Conical Intersect: Sculpture, Space and the Cultural Value of Urban Imagery*. Surrey: Ashgate, 2014.

Myerson, Jeremy and Philip Ross. *Space to Work*. London: Laurence King, 2006.

Naumann, Francis. M. *Marcel Duchamp. The Art of Making Art in the Age of Mechanical Reproduction*. Ghent: Luidon Press, 1999.

Onions, C.T. *The Shorter Oxford English Dictionary. On Historical Principles*. Oxford: Oxford University Press, 1972.

Petzet, Muck and Florian Heilmeyer. *Reduce, Reuse, Recycle*. Germany: Hatje Cantz Verlag, 2012.

Pimlott, Mark. *Without and Within. Essays on Territory & the Interior*. Rotterdam Episode Publishers, 2007.

Rice, Charles. *The Emergence of the Interior*. Oxon: Routledge, 2007.

Robert, Philippe. *Adaptations. New Uses for Old Buildings*. New York: Princeton, 1989.

Rykwert , Joseph. *The Necessity of Artifice*. London: Academy Editions, 1982.

Schittich, Christian. *Building in Existing Fabric: Refurbishment, Extension, New Design*. Basel: Birkhauser, 2004.

Schittich, Christian. *Interior Spaces: Space Light Materials*. Basel: Birkhauser, 2002.

Schneiderman, Deborah. *Inside Prefab: The Ready Made Interior*. New York Princeton Architectural Press, 2012.

Scott, Fred. *On Altering Architecture*. Oxon: Routledge, 2008.

Swinnen, Peter. *51N4E Double or Nothing*. London: AA Publications, 2011.

Tally, Robert T. *Spatiality*. Oxford: Routledge, 2013.

Taylor, Mark and Julieanna Preston. *Intimus—Interior Design Theory Reader*. Chichester: Wiley-Academy, 2006.

Tschumi, Bernard. *Questions of Space*. London: AA Publications, 1990.

Teyssot, Georges. *A Topology of Everyday Constellations*. Boston: MIT Press, 2013.

Venturi, Robert. *Complexity & Contradiction in Architecture*. London: Butterworth Architecture, 1966.

Weinthal, Lois. *Toward a New Interior—An Anthology of Interior Design Theory*. New York: Princeton, 2011.

Wigley, Mark. *White Walls, Designer Dresses. The Fashioning of Modern Architecture*. Boston: MIT Press, 2001.

ARTICLES

"Astley Castle Brief," Witherford Watson Mann press packet.

Branzi, Andrea. "Exhibition Design as Metaphor of a New Modernity Lotus International," *Brooker/Stone Reader*, no. 115 (2002): 162.

Diller, Liz of Diller & Scofidio & Renfro. Interviewed in *Surface Magazine* 113 (Nov. 2014): 128.

Duchamp, Marcel. "Apropos of Ready-mades," 1961. Cited in Evans, David (Ed), (2009), *Appropriation*, London: Whitechapel Gallery Press, 40.

Ging, Jow-Jiun. "Latent Architecture: On Interbreeding Field." http://www.interbreedingfield.com/work.html accessed Feb. 2015.

"Hankai House" Katsuhiro Miyamoto project press packet.

"HAKA-RECYCLE-AN APPROACH FOR STUSTAINABLE INTERIORS" Doepel Strijkers, press packet.

Linn, Charles. "Missouri Bank Branches," www.architectmagazine.com, April 2012, p.107.

"Report on 8B" Arturo Franco Press packet, march 2015.

Rice, C. "Rethinking histories of the interior," *The Journal of Architecture* 9, no. 3 (2004): 275–287.

Riva, Umberto. "Neither an Abandonment nor a Comment." *Abitare Magazine*. March 2013, p. 69.

Sobel, Ralph. "Renovation Beyond Metabolism," *JAPAN ARCHITECT* no. 73 (Spring 2009): 119.

"Universita Station, Naples," Karim Rashid press packet March 2015.

Yabuka, Narelle. "Bright Spark" *Architects Journal Magazine*, June 9, 2012 p. 36.

Acknowledgments

This book would not have been possible without the assistance and support of a number of people. For her research and intelligent systemising of the material from libraries and archives between Milan and London, I would like to say a profound thank you to Dr. Laura Galluzzo. My deepest gratitude goes to all of the designers, photographers and clients who supplied me with images and drawings and their kind permission to use them. Thanks also to Chris Black and his team.

Kate Duffy and Leafy Cummins at Bloomsbury deserve many thanks for their kind and gently persuasive e-mails, particularly around deadline days. I undertook much of this work whilst I was Head of Department of Fashion and Interiors at Middlesex University. Therefore Professor Hilary Robinson, Dr Phil Healy and Professors David Fern and Meg Osborne deserve many thanks for their support, occasional cups of tea and not too many questions about any missed SLT's. Special thanks are reserved for Professor Paul Haywood for his enthusiastic participation in 'The lunch club'.

This book was inspired by *Adaptations*, in my view one of the first rigorous and comprehensive books on building reuse. My thanks and appreciation goes to its author Phillipe Robert. Finally, thanks to Claire and to Mr. Osgood, for their serenity and resilience throughout the duration of this project.

Image Credits